The Secret Life of Decisions

*This book is dedicated to all of my mentors,
those who have disappeared from view but whose wise words live on, and
those around me today who continue to challenge and shape my thinking.*

Meena Thuraisingham

The Secret Life of Decisions

How Unconscious Bias Subverts Your Judgement

MEENA THURAISINGHAM

in collaboration with
WOLFGANG LEHMACHER

GOWER

Published by
Gower Publishing Limited
Wey Court East
Union Road
Farnham
Surrey, GU9 7PT
England

Ashgate Publishing Company
110 Cherry Street
Suite 3-1
Burlington,
VT 05401-3818
USA

www.gowerpublishing.com

British Library Cataloguing in Publication Data
Thuraisingham, Meena.
  The secret life of decisions : how unconscious bias
  subverts your judgement.
  1. Decision making. 2. Judgment. 3. Subconsciousness.
  I. Title
  658.4'03-dc23

  ISBN: 978-1-4094-5327-7 (pbk)
       978-1-4094-5328-4 (ebk)
       978-1-4724-0816-7 (epub)

Library of Congress Cataloging-in-Publication Data
Thuraisingham, Meena.
  The secret life of decisions : how unconscious bias subverts your judgement / by Meena Thuraisingham.
      p. cm.
  Includes bibliographical references and index.
  ISBN 978-1-4094-5327-7 (pbk.) -- ISBN 978-1-4094-5328-4 (ebook)
  1. Decision making. 2. Discrimination--Psychological aspects. 3. Judgment. 4. Leadership. I. Title.
  HD30.23.T48 2013
  153.8'3--dc23

                                                                                    2012035595

Printed and bound in Great Britain by the
MPG Books Group, UK

Contents

List of Figures

Introduction

Making decisions is a critical part of every executive's job, just as it is in our everyday lives. However we know so little about the often subliminal processes that shape the decisions we make, in particular the more critical ones. Seeking to unravel and lay bare the often unchallenged myths and distortions that impact our reasoning ability, this book is intended to raise our awareness and understanding of the many traps we can quite easily fall into. It plumbs the depths of the secret life of decisions.

We are all familiar with the tendency we have to stick with the status quo, or to look for evidence to confirm our preferences or make choices that justify own past choices, throw good money after bad because we find it hard to admit we may be wrong or allowing memorable events in the past to dictate our view of what is possible or likely in the future. These are all examples of the distortions we have all fallen victim to and reflects the all too human aspects of decision making. Most of these 'traps' are dangerous because they are invisible, hardwired into our thinking process in a way that makes it difficult for us to recognise them for what they are. Perhaps more critically we more readily spot the biases of others but not the ones we ourselves bring to the table. By familiarising ourselves with these traps in their many forms, we can make sure that decisions we make are sound and reliable. Awareness is the answer in outing these 'secret' forces that can sabotage the quality of our decisions.

The idea for this book has come from several decades of work with leaders and their teams and the keen observation of how even the most talented leaders can end up making suboptimal decisions, very rarely because they had poor critical thinking faculties or lacked intellect. It was almost always because they did not pay enough attention to the often invisible traps 'set for us' by our brains, letting through only information that conforms with their current beliefs, mental models and expectations. This leaves many leaders and businesses exposed.

From a business perspective, the Global Financial Crisis (GFC), still with us after five years, has brought into question the very basis of how we make decisions; in particular the narrow 'world view' we apply in thinking through business challenges as well as our inability to see past the immediate consequences of our decisions. We continue to apply the optimistic 'I've seen this one before' lens, never challenging the constant reconstructive nature of our memories of events and the ways in which our own experience may place perimeters on our own thinking and subvert our judgements.

While we think of decision making as a rational output of our reasoning abilities, the central premise of this book suggests otherwise. Its premise is that as people are social in nature, their judgements and decisions are subject to social influences. Even when making a decision alone we often tailor our decision behaviours in anticipation to how it will be evaluated by others. Therefore any comprehensive understanding of decision making must examine social influences as they can enhance or hinder decision making. When people are faced with a complicated judgement or decision they often simplify the task by relying on heuristics or general rules of thumb and past experience. In many cases these shortcuts are very close approximations to the optimal answers suggested by decision-making theories, never identical. In certain situations this leads to predictable biases and inconsistencies. We often come to the table armed with our own perspectives, preferences, filters, heuristics and biases, influenced by our upbringing, education, the people we mix with or are exposed to, the religious group we belong to, the media we access and so on.

This book not only explores the major biases that operate and influence the quality of our judgement and the decisions we make, through real stories and scenarios of many leaders we have observed and studied. It also provides the reader with actionable insights through a three-part 'mindset–players–process' framework that helps the decision maker work through the increasingly complex decisions they are called upon to make. And finally the book introduces the reader to a propriety decision diagnostic we have developed that will help leaders reflect on their decision behaviour and choose the changes they wish to make.

This book treats choosing wisely and the thinking involved as a skill, which as with many other skills, can be improved with experience and guided practice.

Note on the Structure of the Book

PART 1: THE COSTS OF BIASED JUDGEMENTS AND BAD DECISIONS

In this part of the book we take a quick and somewhat simplified journey through the physiology and psychology of decision making to help us understand the roots of biased thinking. We also examine the potential business consequences of not addressing this everyday phenomenon more systematically.

PART 2: DEFYING THE MYTHS, REVEALING THE 'SECRETS' AND CHOOSING WISELY

In Part Two we look at the five decisions that every business leader has to make and in that context introduce you to the eight most common decision myths and traps that every business leader needs to watch out for. We look for example at how our over-dependence on numbers can lead us astray, how our discomfort with uncertainty causes us to ignore the unknowables when making a decision and so on. Each chapter alerts to the red flags and provides success strategies that will help neutralise that particular bias. We also provide some coaching strategies for use with the teams or projects you lead.

PART 3: DEVELOPING BEST PRACTICE DECISION BEHAVIOUR

Having accepted that bias is a normal part of human cognitive function, this part of the book distils the insights and ideas from Part 2 into best practice decision behaviour. We also look forward to how decision making is likely to evolve and change. In the future, a new generation of decision makers combined with new value systems and new dynamics (post GFC), globalisation and new technologies may change what we know today about exercising intelligent choice and shape the complex and high stakes business decisions we need to make in the future.

PART I

The Costs of Biased Judgements and Bad Decisions

Thinking About Our Thinking

There is nothing more critical to the success of a business than the quality of judgements and decisions it makes. However the challenge facing decision makers everywhere, even if many may not wish to admit it, is that decision-making behaviour is extremely imprecise. Furthermore we are not as skilled in decision making as we like to believe we are. Besides while we would like to believe that organisations are largely built on ideas of rationality, they in fact operate in irrational ways because it is people that are tasked with making organisations work, and people bring emotions with them.

However even when people appear to act in irrational ways, they are generally irrational in a systematic way, that is ways that are related to their thinking habits. This is why decisions make for fertile ground for much to go wrong – one's personal filters, bias, preferences, values and beliefs get in the way and result in decisions that may not be as skilful as they could be.

Thinking is about sense making. Sir Frederick Bartlett[1] the father of cognitive psychology, working at the University of Cambridge through the 1960s, defined thinking as the skill of filling gaps in evidence. We see a bank up of traffic on a road we know well and think there must be an accident ahead, we hear a tune and think that perhaps it is a piece by Mozart or we read and disagree with a news report, and think the journalist may not have been as thorough in her analysis and so on. It is a picture painted in our minds by our perceptual system and it helps us infer casual relationships and other sense making, through the performance of a mental operation. These perceptual operations happen every second we are awake in everyday life as it does in business.

In essence this 'sense making' comes in two forms of thinking – intuitive or automatic thinking and deductive or analytical thinking. Automatic thinking is pure association. Most of our thinking is associational in nature. For example, we walk into a room and reach for the light switch instinctively without having to think about it believing it will illuminate the room; we bring the car we are driving to a standstill at a red light. We do not think consciously about the actions we are taking – they happen automatically without 'too much thinking'. Controlled thinking is more formal and usually associated with more 'scientific' thinking – a consideration of alternative explanations of what one is confronted with or is experiencing. Any intellectual achievement is always a mixture of both – a combination of intuition and logical deductive processes. Research shows an experienced business leader is likely to be very familiar with a whole range of situations that present themselves to him or her so that they can automatically assess a situation and decide what constitutes a good move or a bad move without 'too much thinking'.

Making judgements and choices via automatic thinking can be useful and efficient but it can also land us into trouble. It can lead us to make poorer judgements and choices that we may not have made if we were employing a more controlled manner about our decisions. This is not to say that intuitive thought is always inferior. As the following chapters will demonstrate, both are important for wise decisions and we refer to this as more mindful thinking, necessary for better decisions.

Finally our cognitive habits are difficult to shake because associations and heuristics are ubiquitous in our thinking processes and in fact necessary for survival. Attempts to train people not to think representatively or overerly on intuition, associations and heuristics are mostly unsuccessful. We therefore have to take precautions against ourselves by investing self-knowledge, self-control and effort in our thinking.

Part II of this book looks closely at the decision behaviour of business leaders, identifies the challenges of making good choices, judgements and decisions; recognises the risks that our own preferences, filters and biases represent and explores ways of modifying our decision behaviours in a way that helps lead the business, decision by decision, to enduring success.

The Roots of Biased Thinking

As business leaders, we face complex decisions where there is really no right or wrong and often on which much is riding. For example, which strategy to

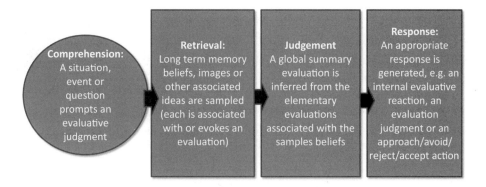

Figure 1.1   The process of making a decision

Source: Adapted from Tourangeau, Rips & Rasinski, 2000[2]

pursue, the market to get out of, the technology platform to invest in for the future, the people to retain or let go and so on.

Irrespective of the type of decision a leader is confronted with, every decision process has effectively four parts as shown in the diagram (Figure 1.1) above:

- comprehension

- retrieval

- judgement

- response.

At every stage, including comprehension, which itself is largely an interpretive action, the decision maker is adding layer upon layer of interpretation and therefore subjectivity. There is also no such thing as context-free decision making. All judgements and decisions rest on the way we see, interpret and choose to comprehend the world around us.

Retrieval is the act of drawing from past experience. That too is influenced and bounded by what the decision maker has previously experienced. It is worth noting that this retrieval process is notoriously unreliable not least because most complex decisions have to be made up of many small evaluations into one global evaluation. For example, the decision to buy or sell a business is made up of many small evaluations – what are the valuations for similar businesses? How is the broader market travelling? Are there particular companies for which this business would be a strategic fit? Is there some perceived value in the business for sale that can be further unlocked, and therefore should we execute those changes before putting the business up for sale? And so on. As Chapters 3 and 4 will show, retrieval is coloured heavily by memory and experience.

In the judgement phase we are drawing on our human ability to infer, estimate or predict the outcome and consequences of unknown events. Our expectations of those outcomes and consequences are also assessed on an evaluative continuum reflecting personal values (the impact of what is valued by the decision maker is examined more closely in Chapter 9) and current goals. Our judgement faculties are subject to certain systematic flaws – the most prominent being overconfidence, explored more fully in Chapter 5. As we get more senior we rely on what got us successfully there and our confidence builds in our own view of how the world works. This confidence can sometimes be extended beyond what is a reasonable level, given the presenting facts of the case.

However, what makes the judgement phase difficult is that in making an intelligent choice of the best course of action, there are many important consequential attributes to consider. As every plus has a negative, every choice comes with a downside and upside and therefore decisions require significant cognitive effort especially if a number of tradeoffs are required (say between competing/conflicting values); even more difficult when critical information is not available to decide on tradeoffs.

Our ability to estimate frequencies, judge similarities, recognise a previously experienced situation, ability to infer causal relationships and so on are all wired into our brain so deeply that it is mostly hardwired. While such intuitive or heuristic thinking is cognitively economical it is also sometimes dangerous or plain stupid. We know one banker and we imagine all others are similar or we do business in one Asian country and we believe that all of Asia operates in similar ways or we meet one Indian and believe that all Indians are pretty much similar in their outlook. Someone who has built his career on successful turnarounds, assuming that every turnaround will be similar, will potentially misjudge badly one that is different.

In Part II we will look at many examples of how this hardwiring can get even the most experienced and successful leaders in trouble often in spectacular ways. Over confidence in one's decision-making skill and optimism about outcomes are therefore two of the biggest dangers leaders face. However as we will show in the following chapters, these are not the only two dangers that lurk for leaders.

Notes

1 *Thinking*, Sir Frederick Bartlett, Allen and Unwin, 1958, with numerous more recent citations.
2 *The Psychology of Survey Response*, R. Tourangeau, L. J. Rips and K. Rasinski, Cambridge University Press, 2000.

2

The Costs of Biased Thinking

One of the tests of a leader's importance is whether anyone is really affected by or cares about the decisions they make. On the assumption that their decisions matter, the leader's legacy is often determined by the long-term impact of their decisions. Therefore the decisions we make are an important part of who we are as leaders.

However as we have seen in Chapter 1, decision making relies on perception and can therefore can be a highly imperfect process. We see what we expect to see, that is, we observe selectively; we interpret events so as to confirm our view noticing only information that is consistent with our world views and ignoring dissonant information; we often remember things that did not happen or at least not the way we remember them. This leaves leaders and organisations exposed and out of touch in a number of ways, and in turn the decisions they make.

In this chapter we show how costly biased thinking can be. We also show through well-documented examples how even the most experienced and successful companies and leaders can fall victim to the following eight myths.

The Memory Myth: An Accurate Memory of Past Events is a Reliable Input into Our Decisions (Chapter 3)

Many of the judgements and decisions we make in business today are based on our recall of accumulated knowledge and expertise. But as scientists have shown our recollections are often imperfect.

The *Ebbinghaus Curve of Forgetting* developed by cognitive scientists during the 1970s and 1980s (following original research by a German psychologist Herman Ebbinghaus) shows how the natural process of memory constitutes some forgetting because memory is a reconstruction. It is also reassembled across multiple regions of the brain (a process we are not conscious of) when it is recalled, reconstructed and is accompanied by a strong sense of knowing.

In numerous experiments by cognitive scientists, this curve was tested against people's memories of national tragedies such as J. F. Kennedy's shooting, *Challenger*'s crash and more recently 9/11, the day after it happened and again at regular intervals and three years later. Most of us will remember what scientists call 'flashbulb memories' – so called because of their stunning vivid detail which erodes over time at the same rate as our everyday recollections. Their research shows that less than 7 per cent of recollections match the initial event, 50 per cent were wrong in two-thirds of their assertions and 25 per cent were wrong in every major detail. The results for everyday events are generally similar in terms of memory accuracy as with 'flashbulb memories'.

Our memories as we can see (even for large significant events) are riddled with errors of detail. What is more interesting is how these memories continue to feel so right and are accompanied with such a blinding conviction. Our own certainty is often taken as an indicator of accuracy.

On Monday August 29, 2005, Hurricane Katrina hit the south coast of America, 55 miles south of New Orleans – a heavily populated city much of which was below sea level.

General Matthew Broderick, Director of the 300 staff-strong Homeland Security Operations Centre, Washington DC (which was the clearing hub for intelligence from the ground on major domestic disasters before passing it on to the White House) was an experienced man in charge at the time of Katrina. He had 30 years of experience running the Operations Centre of the Marine Corps including the evacuation of Saigon and Phnom Penh. If anyone was qualified to sift good information from bad, Broderick was. However his long experience had told him that first reports are often inaccurate and exaggerated. So he spent that Monday trying to get confirmation from reliable reports on whether the levies of New Orleans had been breached. Reports were coming in thick and fast and by the end of the day he had many reports, some of which were conflicting, and he had to decide the reliability of those reports. That evening he went home after reassuring the White House that there was no substantial breach of New Orleans levies. It was not until late morning on the August 30 when he informed the White House that levies had been breached and much of New Orleans was already under water. This delayed the federal response by 24 hours causing the death of 1,800 people and hundreds and thousands to lose their homes and livelihoods. Katrina was a disaster that cost the US Federal Government US$86 billion.

In that critical 24-hour period after the hurricane had hit the south coast, Broderick had listened to those reports carefully, selectively picking a few that appeared to him as less exaggerated, all the time applying his recollection of how the first reports of previous events he had managed had been exaggerated. He failed to notice the one to two reports that held the truth of what was unfolding.

'It's my responsibility ... to inform these key personnel,' Broderick told a Senate panel investigating the Katrina response. 'If they did not receive ... information, it was my responsibility and my fault.' He later resigned citing family reasons.

We all have 'Broderick moments' when we missed a vital clue because we engaged in selective listening and selective recall, compounded by our very own *Ebbinghaus Curve of Forgetting*.

This decision myth and the impact of the underlying memory bias is explored fully in Chapter 3.

The Experience Myth: The More Experience We Have the Better our Decisions (Chapter 4)

Knowing what we don't know is often seen as the beginning of real wisdom. In spite of this we can allow our own experience to limit our field of vision and this is especially true in the case of Microsoft and its CEO Steve Ballmer (who is employee number 30 at Microsoft and can claim over 30 years of continued employment with the same company).

Underestimating his competition and tied to the 20-year head start in software that Microsoft had over its competition, Ballmer is now famous for saying of the iPhone:

> There's no chance that the iPhone is going to get any significant market share. No chance. It's a $500 subsidized item. They may make a lot of money. But if you actually take a look at the 1.3 billion phones that get

sold, I'd prefer to have our software in 60% or 70% or 80% of them,
than I would to have 2% or 3%, which is what Apple might get.

However it was not only market potential in phone technology that Microsoft underestimated.

By 1998 a prototype of a Microsoft electronic reader which would allow customers to download digital versions of any written material was ready to go. However the working group who developed this prototype was given the thumbs down because it did not look like Windows. In spite of the team arguing that the point was to have a book, and a book alone, appear on the full screen and putting it into an electronic version would do nothing but undermine the consumer experience, they were drowned out. The working group was subsequently folded into the Major Products Group dedicated to software for Office – the cash cow. It is not hard to see why Amazon and Apple were able to conquer the e-book reader market some years later.

It seemed that Microsoft was too tied to Windows and Office. Every idea that talented groups came up with had to be built off Windows or other existing product. There were all sorts of biases at work here, principally the experience and attachment biases. For example Office was designed for inputting with a keyboard, not a stylus or a finger. Thinking continued to be tied to the keyboard. The trouble with biases such as this keyboard bias was that the problems Microsoft's young innovators were trying to solve were not ones relating to Microsoft product. In spite of that they had to fit their thinking into how Microsoft worked which slowed down and crushed the innovation process. Biases at every level permeated the company, with Windows and Office divisions dictating the direction of product development, leaving the company unable to move quickly when faced with a rapidly changing market place.

It is one thing to underestimate new entrants but quite another to underestimate the ambition of your competitors. More generally, it has been clear for some time now that the shift to mobile devices and cloud architecture is reducing the need, and desire, for PCs in homes, offices and data centres. Microsoft appears years late in recognising this seismic market shift, bounded in their thinking about the market they so effectively once led. They allowed themselves to become victims of their own experience. Microsoft's flagging share price over the past decade now reflects this clearly.

Microsoft is a great example of being bounded by one's own experience – something that many large industry incumbents fall into the trap of. A way of doing things that can become so entrenched it is hard to see past that success. Having had a 20-year run with Windows did not mean that this software domination would continue.

In every field the expert view or the voice of experience constitutes a filter – a highly focused perception that is based on a finite body of knowledge and rarely includes a paranoid view of the world. Every time we use a filter of experience we discard part of the total picture.

This decision myth and the impact of the underlying experience bias is explored fully in Chapter 4.

The Optimism Myth: The More Confident We Feel About the Outcome the Better Our Decisions (Chapter 5)

The tendency to drive through with action on something over which others may hesitate is common. It comes from an overconfidence about two things:

- our ability to impact or influence the future;

- our ability to predict the future.

The numerous times you may have witnessed the missing of a budget, either your own or others' budgets, points to the fact that this overconfidence or optimism is often misplaced.

There is something implicit in the way organisations are structured around competence that encourages optimism. Executives are put in charge of markets or portfolios because they are deemed to have what it takes. It is therefore a rare occurrence to observe the humility of a leader who stands in front of their CEO or Board and conveys their level of uncertainty about the plan he/she is propagating. They would rarely be heard saying why their plan may not work. It is the job of an executive to present confidently about their plan and inspire confidence and optimism in others. In fact they will routinely spend time talking up the plan while covering off the risks and the potential hazards. Additionally their treatment of these risks and hazards usually demonstrates their confidence in their ability to predict how the market will react. Added to this, there is a tendency to assume that what happened before will happen again.

In fact many organisational cultures appear to survive on optimism, suppressing uncertainty along the way. The Global Financial Crisis (GFC) personified the optimism of all its players leading into the collapse of Bear Sterns' in early 2008. The collapse of the company was a prelude to the risk management meltdown of the Wall Street investment banking industry in September 2008, and the subsequent GFC and recession. This collapse was one fuelled by optimism and has been documented extensively since 2008.

Particularly when under pressure, executives are more likely to push ahead on assumptions which will later on prove to be wrong. This is often fuelled by the confidence we have in our own ability to accurately predict the future. However, this prediction is often based on sources of information and knowledge on which we draw selectively, using the filters of memory and experience described earlier in this chapter.

This decision myth and the impact of the underlying optimism bias is explored fully in Chapter 5.

The Fear Myth: The More We Have to Lose the Better Our Decisions (Chapter 6)

Our fear of failing or losing something can cause us to make dumb decisions. In the case of Kodak, its fear of cannibalising its own film business turned it away from a new important technology forever changing the course of the company's history.

Kodak, a pioneering company, invented amateur photography and was rewarded with decades of profitable revenue growth as its string of cheap cameras, film products and photographic papers changed the way people thought about photographs. It was then the world leader in photographic film and paper sales, and, with great margins, its value grew exponentially. However in the late 1980s, when digital imaging was introduced, amateur photography went digital which meant no more film, and no need for developing film.

What is not commonly known however is that Kodak invented digital photography, creating the technology, and were in fact the first to apply it. But because of fears they would cannibalise their film sales, the then executive management made a decision not to market it. In an effort to defend and extend their old business, Kodak licensed digital photography patents to camera manufacturers, abandoned research and development (R&D) in the product line and maintained their focus on the core business. Kodak kept making amateur film better, faster and cheaper – eventually driving themselves into competitive extinction – the real cost of their fear.

In early 2012, Kodak filed for chapter 11 bankruptcy.

This decision myth and the impact of the underlying fear bias is explored fully in Chapter 6.

The Ambition Myth: The Stronger Our Personal Ambition the Better Our Decisions (Chapter 7)

Ambition is among the strongest and most creative forces in the world and frequently the reason things get done. While it can drive you to be better, get more, be first, be biggest and so on, it is also one of the most dangerous forces if unchecked. Left unchecked, ambition can cross the line, becoming arrogance and avarice. Hubris is not far behind, driven not by ambition for the enterprise but ambition for self, ultimately leading to self-destruction.

Such hubris can blindside us as it did with Fred Goodwin the disgraced CEO of RBS (the Royal Bank of Scotland). His long track record of leveraged buy-outs on both sides of the Atlantic (including the purchase of NatWest in 2000, a company three times the size of RBS at the time) held many clues of the hubris that accompanied his final move – the purchase of ABN Amro for which he paid too much. He took decisions that ignored prudent advice on the balance between capital and assets, leaving RBS undercapitalised and soon after causing it to become nationalised in order to not bring down the UK economy with it.

All the time his ambition was to build the world's largest company which Goodwin succeeded in doing in 2008 when he presided over RBS's rapid rise to global prominence as the world's largest company (by assets – £1.9 trillion), and fifth-largest bank by stock market value. He resigned a month before RBS announced the largest loss in UK corporate history, some £24 billion. This was the true cost of his ambition and his failure to wisely judge the challenges associated with building a sustainable enterprise.

It is now known that those who knew and worked for him advised caution. His ambition however was a driving force, many recognising this trait. Some admired it while others saw it as hubris. He projected a sense of self-assurance that mesmerised his followers, and although unsettling his detractors, he gave the impression that he always knew where he was going and what he was going to do when he got there. That impression eventually proved to be his undoing as it mutated into an imperious arrogance and hubris that cost him his job, his career and much of his life, not to mention the tens of thousands of employees and customers who relied on RBS.

This decision myth and impact of the underlying ambition bias is explored fully in Chapter 7.

The Attachment Myth: The More Emotion We Have Vested in Ideas or People the Better Our Decisions (Chapter 8)

Even when we make decisions on our own we often consider how others may receive our decisions. The very human questions like, 'Would they feel betrayed?' 'Would she be disappointed?' 'Would he feel misled?' 'Would they blame me?' 'Would my team think I am doing a back-flip?' and so on.

You can form attachments to a person, a group of people, a shared history but also to strategies, ideas or even iconic brands. Such attachments or affiliations can influence the quality of decisions. Business literature is scattered with examples of executives who looked through the attachment lens and made bad decisions, in particular executives who, on the principle of sunk costs, continued to stay attached to a strategy that had run its course.

In 2001, McDonald's announced a major restructuring after many quarters of declining profits, climbing debt and a stock price falling 60 per cent in three years. Leading up to this point, the only strategy that they pursued was opening more stores (rather than improving existing ones). They fell victim to the attachment bias – attached to a single strategy for growth, that is, more new stores.

Despite owning a brand that was the sixth most recognised in the world, the preceding decade was one of disappointing performance in terms of declining profits and poor stock performance. More importantly lower taste ranking compared to competitors, dissident franchisees and changed recipes to cut costs were driving customers away.

The then Chairman/CEO Michael Quinlan was asked in a Newsweek interview if change was needed. He said, 'Do we have to change? No we don't need to change, we have the most successful brand in the world.' The illusion of vulnerability and collective rationalisation had crept into the organisation but most of all they had fallen victim to an attachment to a single strategic frame, a way of growing that became a dominant logic.

Eventually they got a new leader, with fresh ideas and an open mind, a leader who quickly shifted the strategy away from the company's traditional attachment and reliance on growth through opening new units to improving existing stores and generating more sales from existing stores. This unemotional approach to what was needed was the key to McDonald's turnaround. They were finally able to challenge and neutralise this (attachment) bias.

This decision myth and the impact of the underlying attachment bias is explored fully in Chapter 8.

The Values Myth: The Stronger the Corporate Culture or Belief System the Better Our Decisions (Chapter 9)

Our singular commitment to a set of values or beliefs can blindside us in ways that can have catastrophic consequences as in the case of Alan Greenspan, the five-term Fed chief feted by every commentator and regularly referred to as 'the greatest banker in history'. His fame extended beyond the US – he was awarded the French Legion of Honour and Britain made him an Honorary Knight. When in October 2008 he finally appeared before a Committee of the US House of Representatives to testify during an investigation into the financial crisis, every kind of crisis was starting to unfold. First there was the subprime mortgage crisis which led to a liquidity crisis followed by a credit crisis, a banking crisis, a currency crisis and then a trade crisis. But more critically this collapse of the global economy heralded an ideological crisis as well, underpinned by a single model of how markets could or should work.

Greenspan's model of how markets will work is that they will regulate themselves. This was a belief that was unshakable and adopted by many financiers as Michael Lewis's books will attest to. Waxman, one of the committee members, offered Greenspan an explanation at the inquiry when he struggled to explain what had happened – 'You found your view of the world, your ideology was not right.' Greenspan relied, 'Precisely. That was precisely the reason I was shocked, because I had been going for 40 years or more with very considerable evidence that it was working exceptionally well,'

Greenspan was shocked, but not because he was never warned of it, countless people did challenge his deregulatory dogma including Nobel Prize winning economists. In fact he took the extraordinary step of silencing one of them by convincing the US Congress to pass legislation preventing the then Head of the Commodity Futures Trading Commission – Brooksley Born – an economist who had called for the regulation of the market for derivatives, citing 'grave concerns about the consequences' of such regulation. Greenspan's confidence in his model of how the world worked was absolute and unshakeable.

We all have 'Greenspan moments' when we hold something to be true and core to our beliefs, ignoring evidence that may suggest the contrary until of course something calamitous happens and we are suddenly struck by how that set of beliefs or values could have blinded us or led us away from the very success we were aiming at.

Burston Marstellar and News Corp are examples of companies who had made decisions that were shaped by their values and beliefs but ended up unintentionally causing irreparable damage to their reputations.

This decision myth and impact of the underlying values bias is explored fully in Chapter 9.

The Power Myth: The More Control or Influence We Have the Better Our Decisions (Chapter 10)

Our reliance on vested power can prevent us from challenging our own thinking, surrounding ourselves with people who support our view or at least don't challenge us which in turn further cements our view. CEOs who rule by position power eventually fail. It usually takes some precipitating event

– a strategic mistake, a falling stock price, a whiff of scandal – to create the conditions for such personal failure to occur.

Possibly the most brutal of all oustings of a sitting CEO at a large public company was CEO of Morgan Stanley, Philip Purcell. Purcell's detractors found voice because of a wave of high-profile executive departures (who could not work with him), a lagging share price and uncertain profit outlook. But these appeared to be mere symptoms reputedly of a deeper issue relating to how key decisions got made at Morgan Stanley; how Purcell used power to rule, instil obedience, demand loyalty and mete out revenge for those suspected of having split loyalties.

Reportedly, his Machiavellian style, characterised by ruthlessness, autocracy and aloofness, was blamed for many of the top executives departing. After becoming CEO in 1997, he was tasked with having to integrate a top-end investment banking franchise (Morgan Stanley) and a retail brokerage network (Dean Witter from where Purcell came) into a single integrated financial services firm. During the integration, he reportedly showed no tolerance for dissent or even argument, surrounding himself with 'yes men' and 'yes women', demanding loyalty to himself over the organisation. Furthermore it was reported at the time that he alienated the firm from its regulators, managing to upset them with his high-handed and arrogant style on a range of issues the firm was facing in the courts at that time.

Even towards the end of his tenure, when the Board undertook their own independent interviews of executives reporting to Purcell to find out what was really going on, Purcell refused to accept responsibility for both flagging morale and for the lack of firm cohesion. A very long and punishing two-month public campaign ensued, waged in the media by a group of eight departed executives calling for Mr Purcell's exit. The Board, initially misjudging attacks on Mr Purcell by former executives as a personal vendetta rather than an issue that threatened the company's performance, finally abandoned their longstanding support of Purcell and took action to remove him.

Morgan Stanley, under Purcell, was evidently demoralised by a decision-making style that was based on power not influence. John J. Mack, who had been pushed out in a power struggle some four years previously, was subsequently installed by the Board as the CEO.

This decision myth and impact of the underlying power bias is explored fully in Chapter 10.

In Summary

In illustrating the costs of biased thinking, we used well-documented and high-profile examples of leaders and companies that fell victim to these eight decision-making myths and underlying biases, showing clearly how costly the impact of the biased decisions can be. But these are not one-off examples as we will demonstrate in Part II of this book.

Through our business and consulting experience over the past three decades we have gathered hundreds of examples of leaders who have fallen victim to these biases. We will bring these dangers to life with examples that draw from that experience to show that you may be succumbing to some of those distortions even in the decisions you are making today.

Knowledge is key, as we are not consciously aware of the frames of reference, rules of thumb and preferences that are hardwired into our brains. This lack of knowledge causes our judgements to be far from accurate, not thoughtful enough, emotionally and culturally driven and has the potential of destroying our credibility as decision makers.

However before we despair about how exposed we are in what is the truly imprecise process of making decisions, there is hope.

Some of this hope resides in that fact that these 'errors' can be identified by better knowledge, careful mindful observation and practice and acted on by informed choice and some very simple skills that every leader can acquire. In Part II we present these skills in a simple framework (see Figure 2.1) that will help you challenge the myths, side step the many traps and correct for the biases, become a better decision maker and ultimately a better leader.

Each of the following chapters culminates with red flags that help the decision maker recognise when the decision-making process may be compromised or distorted. Where this danger is recognised to exist, the decision maker rethinks the mindset, the players or the process in order to generate a more successful decision-making strategy.

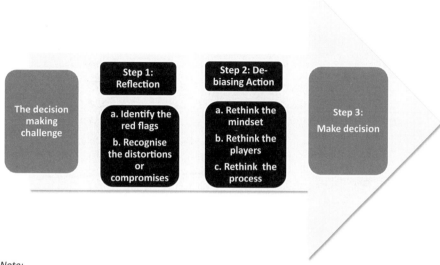

Note:

Each chapter culminates with red flags that help the decision maker recognise when the decision making process may be compromised or distorted. Where this danger is seen to exist, the decision maker rethinks the mindset, the players or the process in order to generate a successful decision making strategy

Figure 2.1   Decision-making framework

PART II

Defying the Myths, Revealing the 'Secrets' and Choosing Wisely

Introduction to Part II

First let's take a short journey through the history of flawed thinking, judgment and consequent decisions:

> *I think there is a world market for maybe five computers.*
>
> *Thomas Watson JR, Head of IBM 1956–1970*

> *Who the hell wants to hear actors talk?*
>
> *Harry M Warner, Warner Brothers, 1927*

> *We don't like their sounds. Groups of guitars are on their way out.*
>
> *Decca Records rejecting The Beatles, 1962*

> *Television won't be able to hold on to any market it captures in the first 6 months. People will soon get tired of staring at a plywood box every night.*
>
> *Daryl F Zanuck, Head of 20th Century Fox, 1946*

Everything that can be invented has been invented.

Charles H Duell, Commissioner of Patents, 1899

While many of these judgements now look ridiculous, as with these judgments we have only hindsight and history to help reveal how wrong we were.

In this part of the book we will examine more closely the way in which we see what we see, interpret what we see, make predictions based on our interpretations and then base our judgments and decisions on those very personalised mental models of how the world works. We refer to this as the 'secret life' of decisions, because of its invisible nature and because it is an aspect of decision making that is rarely outed either by us or by those vested in our decisions, except with hindsight. Without exposing this 'secret life' we will continue to make decisions, in some cases with catastrophic consequences, for the teams and businesses we lead.

However in order to see the business relevance and damage that these myths can wreak on the quality of judgment and decisions, we need to look more closely at the critical challenges that leaders in business today have to master. We see these as five decision challenges:

- Building strategic clarity and coherence (**what is our mission**);
  - judge where the world and company's markets are heading and framing a vision of how the company should reposition itself.

- Picking and developing the right team (**who to pick as team**);
  - identify (and if needed recruit) the talent that can turn that vision into reality.

- Engaging stakeholders (**who should matter**);
  - knowing comprehensively how the company really works and engaging all of its stakeholders openly and constructively for long-term mutual benefit.

- Leading and driving change (**what must change**);
  - take the difficult decisions necessary to remove the barriers to success.

- Risk proofing the organisation (**what are the risks**);
  - understand in a deep and substantive way the problems that the company faces to ensure its sustainability.

However, in navigating through these five decisions, we must recognise the 'secret' forces at play. These forces operate pretty much at an unconscious or subconscious level, so we are unaware of the impact they may have in the choices we make. Much like an iceberg, neither we nor recipients of our decisions see the 'secrets' below the water line, rife with bias.

In summary, we reveal eight decision myths (Figure i2.1) that subvert and distort judgement and show these below along with the accompanying risk (graded as high, medium and low) (Figure i2.2) that they pose for the five core decisions all leaders are called on to make. Each chapter in this section will examine these in detail using case examples drawn from our consulting practice and give you strategies to counter these biases and reduce the decision risks you may be unconsciously carrying. The sooner we become aware of these 'secret' forces the better placed we are in making smarter choices and better decisions.

Chapter	The Myth	The Reality
3	An accurate memory of past events is a reliable input to our decisions	Memories can deceive us
4	The more experience we have the better our decisions	Experience can trap us
5	The more confident we are of the outcome the better our decisions	Optimism can cloud
6	The more we have to lose the better our decisions	Fear can do more harm
7	The stronger our personal ambition the better our decisions	Ambition can blindside
8	The more emotion vested in ideas or people the better our decisions	Attachments can lead us astray
9	The stronger the corporate culture or belief system the better our decisions	Values can blindside
10	The more control or influence we have the better our decisions	Power can corrupt

Figure i2.1   Summary of myths and risks to decision makers

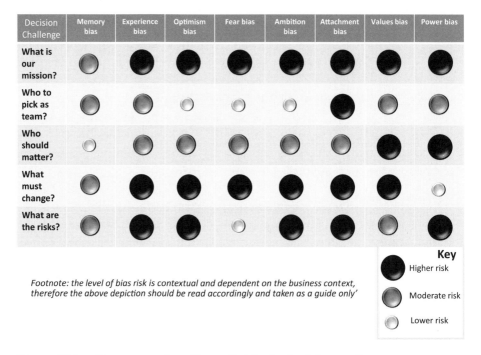

Figure i2.2   Summary of myths and risks to decision makers

Even though these biases are presented in individual chapters, they should not be thought of as able to be categorised in neat discrete boxes but as inter-related in complex ways as the chosen case examples illustrate.

Let's now expose and scrutinise the secret life of decisions more closely…

3

Memories Can Deceive

Challenging the myth that our accurate memories of past events are a reliable input into our decisions.

Psychologist Tali Shalot has shown convincingly how unreliable our memories can be. In her book, *Optimism Bias*, she recounts her study of eyewitness memories of the terrorist attack on September 11, 2001, in New York City. She was intrigued by the fact that people felt their memories were as accurate as a videotape. Often they were riddled with errors. A survey conducted around the US showed that 11 months after the attacks, individuals' recollections of their experience that day were consistent with their initial accounts (given in September 2011) only 63 per cent of the time. They were also poor at remembering details of the event, such as the names of the airline carriers. Even more interestingly they were adamant about their recollections. Where did these mistakes in memory come from?

As our memories are not exact carbon copies of our past experiences but rather constructed at the time of recall, the materials used in this split second reconstruction are logical inferences that fill in missing details, associated memories that blend in with the original memory and other relevant information. We apply heuristics or rules of thumb (our understanding of how the world works) to recall from the detail of that memory, which in turn opens it to all sorts of personalised interpretations at the time of recall. If the information in our memory is biased then it is obvious that our memory-based judgements are biased. We have to therefore apply some judicious mindful thinking to de-bias decisions that draw on memory recall.

These biased reconstructions are not limited to personal experiences, they are also rampant in business today.

The Challenge

Our 'rebuilt' picture of events never reflects the actual event. To illustrate this, do this simple exercise. Close your eyes and recall a scene in which you experienced something pleasurable. Don't read any further until you have finished replaying it in your mind. Did you see yourself in it? Most people do. If you saw yourself in it then you must have reconstructed it unless of course you were looking at yourself during the original experience.

The feeling that accompanied an event, and the meaning we subsequently attach to it, is also very much part of that memory. Our memory of the experience acts as a filter for our perception of the world and as such the same experience is remembered by each of us in very different ways. This is why when an executive encounters failure or setback (accompanied by anger, hurt, disappointment, grief and so on), they may often selectively remember their part in it and then fail to draw the right lessons from it. They commit into their 'rebuilt' memory a greater prominence of attributing factors such as luck or external factors. Such mental strategies help us to ensure our impunity in a given failure. Irrespective of our motives, our recall morphs into something that is no longer an accurate one.

Memory distortion research now shows how open our memories (however simple or complex) are to interpretation. In fact it is now clear from the last three decades of memory research that people's memories are not just a sum total of all that they have done. It is a sum total of that plus what they have thought they experienced, what they have been told and what they believe. As we will see, not only do we frequently allow post event rationalisation to 'taint' the memory in a self-serving way, but we also have a remarkable capacity for assimilating into memory 'facts' that are consistent with our prevailing notions of 'how the world is meant to be'.

Memory is relevant to every business decision we make. Many of the judgements we make are memory-based in the sense that we don't have the information or data necessary to make the judgements right in front of us. Consequently, we draw from learnt information in the past that is now stored in our long-term memory and that we think is relevant to that judgement. Despite memory being a reconstruction and our recall influenced by many biasing factors, we trust our memories with unquestioning conviction.

As we retrieve and reconstruct memories in business today, distortions can creep in without explicit external influence, and these can become pieces of misinformation. Misinformation comes in many subtle forms and often in forms that we are not conscious of. When witnesses to an event talk with one another, when they are interrogated with leading questions or suggestive techniques, when they see media coverage about an event, misinformation can enter consciousness and can cause contamination of memory. These are not, of course, the only source of bias or distortion in memory. We will look at the full range of distortions in the following section.

A Closer Look

Cognitive science and studies of the brain show that we draw on our memory stores and there are three parts to this store:

- Sensory store – where incoming sensory information is received and transformed over a span of a few seconds.

- Short-term store – a limited short-term working memory where most of conscious thinking occurs.

- Long-term store – a more capacious long-term memory where we store concepts, images, facts, procedures and mental heuristics (one might call our cognitive toolbox) – acquired over a lifetime of making judgements.

Furthermore, our memories (both the short term and long term) are limited by two principles:

- Capacity – information is encoded in more or less efficient ways and this acts to decrease or increase what is recalled, that is, memory capacity.

- Interpretation – the coding process itself depends on the meaning attached to the information, and holds both information as well as the associations we make with the retained information.

In other words our memories are influenced by how much the brain can hold and the interpretations we give to those events (post event). Therefore, our memory of events, their interpretations and extrapolation to further events are influenced by factors other than their accuracy. The predictions we make on which our decisions are based, are generated from a limited, fallible and incomplete system held together by the meaning we give to our experience of events.

Psychologists and cognitive scientists who study memory claim that memories are susceptible to inaccuracies partly because the neural system responsible for remembering episodes from our past might not have evolved for memory alone. The implication of this is that rather than being a system designed to perfectly replay past events, it ends up being influenced by our predictions and expectations, reconstructed such that some details that don't 'fit' are deleted and others inserted.

These experts show that our memories are malleable and can be distorted and biased in a number of ways:

- the impact of misinformation on recall;

- the impact of framing on recall;

- the impact of association on recall;

- the impact of emotion on recall;

- the impact of self-identity on recall;

- the impact of timing/sequencing on recall.

One of the most prominent experts in the faults and flaws of memory is Elizabeth Loftus[1] who started work in the 1970s on the fallibility of our memories. She showed that far from an accurate record, memory is influenced by subsequent exposure to information and events and is reconstituted according to the bias these create. Her earliest studies of eyewitness testimony addressed several issues:

- When someone sees a crime or accident, how accurate is his or her memory?

- What happens when witnesses are questioned by police officers?

- What if those questions are biased?

Her work has now gone beyond the lab and she is regularly called as expert witness in some of the world's most renowned criminal cases (including the Rodney King beatings, the Michael Jackson case, the Bosnian War trials in the Hague and the Oklahoma City bombings). Now a professor, Loftus teaches at the University of California in both the Psychology and Law departments. She argues convincingly about the fallibility of our recollections and memories using as evidence the numerous convictions that have been overturned in America following DNA evidence, sometimes after decades of incarceration.

Let's look at these many memory-related biases more closely.

THE IMPACT OF MISINFORMATION ON RECALL

Misinformation (people are fed with) can cause people to falsely believe that they saw details that were only suggested to them. Misinformation can even lead people to have very rich false memories which once embraced can be expressed with confidence and rich detail.

Loftus and others show how easy it is to create a false memory for a recent event both in the case of simple as well as complex events. These experiments used a simple procedure. Participants first see a complex event such as a simulated motorcar accident. Next, half the participants receive misleading information about the accident whereas the other half do not receive any misinformation. Finally all the participants are asked to try and remember the original accident. In one such experiment participants viewed the accident and later some received misinformation about the traffic sign used to control the intersection. The misled participants got the false suggestion that the stop sign that they had actually seen was a yield sign. When asked later what kind of traffic sign they personally remembered seeing at the intersection those who had the false information tended to adopt it as their memory and now claimed that they had actually seen a yield sign. Those who had not received the misinformation had much more accurate memories. Many experiments following this one showed people remembering broken glass when there was none, a blue car in the accident as white and so on. These experiments show that if an individual is fed (unknowingly) with misinformation, it can change their recollection in predictable and sometimes very powerful ways.

The implication of this for business today is critical in that we base many of our decisions on information. Should some of this information be inaccurate or incomplete, we most certainly cannot rely on our malleable memories to save us from distorted or corrupt recall. Additionally, as we are seldom aware of the nature of the complex distortions that are taking place in our brains in the process of recall, we are sometimes unable to pin-point the risks and therefore unable to mitigate those risks.

THE IMPACT OF FRAMING ON RECALL

Misinformation fed to unsuspecting individuals is not the only way memories are distorted. Leading questions is another powerful way in which our memories can be distorted.

Our memory of events appears to be influenced by post event information such as suggestion or the way questions may be framed. Eyewitness testimony is a great illustration of our ability to recall accurately as it is clear that our recall can be influenced especially in the way questions are asked to illicit information about the event.

Loftus's subjects in an experiment[2] witnessed a film of a car accident and then questioned about details. Two questions were asked:

- Did you see *a* broken headlight?

- Did you see *the* broken headlight?

The first question implied some doubt about the presence of a broken headlight. In this experiment it was found that once a broken headlight was suggested, it became integrated into the memory and recalled as such, even when there was no broken headlight.

This kind of framing effect has been demonstrated by many studies and shown to operate in very subtle ways. For example, when asked how fast the cars were going when they smashed into each other, and the word 'smashed' replaced with 'bumped' into each other or 'contacted' or 'collided', the estimation of speed was materially influenced. This demonstrates how powerfully a single word can distort the accuracy of our recall, fundamentally altering one's reconstructed memory.

The impact of suggestive framing of this kind has significant impact on decision making in business today such that the memory-based decisions may be materially biased by how questions or issues are framed or defined. This may sometimes lead the unsuspecting decision maker towards a suboptimal decision.

THE IMPACT OF ASSOCIATION ON RECALL

Experiments also show that people don't just memorise and store sentences from conversations they hear, they construct and memorise a general scenario where pieces of associated information are integrated with one another and it is difficult to know what came before and what was already known. Often this reconstruction is driven by the meaning we attach to or associate with the event. Sometimes this includes an element of protecting ourselves, for example, our face, ego or to ensure coherence with our personal narratives of how life should be, a phenomenon we examine later in this chapter.

In an experiment conducted by Loftus and her colleagues, they showed subjects a false advertisement for Disneyland which featured the cartoon character Bugs Bunny. Subjects were asked to simply evaluate the ad against a variety of characteristics. Sixteen per cent later claimed they had personally met Bugs Bunny. This was clearly not the case as Bugs Bunny is a Warner Brothers character and would have been nowhere near Disneyland. In fact of those who recalled seeing Bugs Bunny, 62 per cent said they shook his hand, 46 per cent said they remembered hugging him and others remembered touching his ear or tail. This level of sensory detail of an imagined event was not only built into the memories, it showed how easy it was to swap the more accurate 'associative category' relating to the companies that created the characters, with the one relating to cartoon characters in general, with another more accurate one relating to the companies that had created the characters.

We can all recall attending a meeting and coming away from it with a completely different view of what was discussed or decided (from someone else who also attended the same meeting). Often this recall is influenced by the associations we make. We tend to personally recall conversations relating to what we regard as critical with greater accuracy than those ideas or solutions we may not regard as critical. Some may call this selective listening. We also subconsciously overlay on that recall heuristics or rules of thumb with a complex tapestry of assumptions about how the world works, in order to recall from that memory. That is to say that our recall in such a meeting is influenced by associations we make based on our model of how the world works. That is to say, we don't just selectively listen, we also selectively recall. This is the reason why at the end of every decision-making meeting some important protocols have to be observed to ensure the impact of memory and our heuristics don't get in the way of the integrity of committed decisions.

THE IMPACT OF EMOTION ON RECALL

The pleasure and pain we associate with a memory is also an important biasing factor and often referred to as the saliency effect. Some of this is wired in so deeply and occurs so rapidly such that we often have difficulty describing the basis for these feelings. Instead, we may quite automatically distance ourselves from something because of the pain it brought us the last time and the pain it could potentially bring us this time without consciously recognising the basis for such fears. To others this reaction may seem wholly irrational.

Research shows that while we are prone to rewrite history such that distressing events in the past become less and less intense over time and joys we have experienced are often embellished, negative events have more saliency. That is to say we remember negative events better/more often (than positive events) which leads to overestimating the frequency and the probability of such events occurring. Put simply, if an executive challenged the CEO in a previous role which did not go well, for example they got sidelined and then let go, the memory of the trauma and pain associated with that difficult departure is likely to be recalled and intensified. In a subsequent role that executive will subconsciously (and quite irrationally in the view of observers) distance themselves from situations that carry any personal or career risk and may become irrationally cautious about pushing back on or disagreeing with anyone in a more senior role even when they have all the reasons to do so. In fact the memory of that one traumatic event in the past can even result in lasting changes in personal style driven by self-preservation. But while we are all driven by self-preservation, the saliency of this memory causes this executive to exaggerate the risks and downsides in their minds, allowing their decisions to be biased by the trauma they have attached to that memory. This contrasts with the more optimistic view/bias we hold when contemplating our own skills, capabilities and achivements, which we will examine more closely in Chapter 5.

THE IMPACT OF SELF-IDENTITY ON RECALL

Memories are critical to our ability to create both a self-identity and autobiographical history. Memory research shows that autobiographical memories are seldom static, evolving over time. In fact some of our memories are revised over time so as to create a new twist in the narrative or an almost new story line in order to ensure it aligns with our beliefs about who we are and what we stand for.

Not only do memories speak to us of the past, they also guide us in the present and in the anticipated future. We ordinarily think of memories as something we just have, not as something that is transformative of who we are. But as Dr Ethel Person shows, our memories are living, breathing, organs of change. Dr Ethel Person, Professor of Clinical Psychiatry at the Columbia University researches the way we allow beliefs to modify our memories. In her research she demonstrates how we often reinterpret our memories of major events in order to tell a 'better story' about ourselves, especially to ourselves. For example, we may re-edit our memories in response to a divorce or to a promotion that did not materialise. Dr Person also demonstrates how in this re-editing we may cherish something now we devalued in the past, or devalue something now that we cherished in the past. Additionally in the way we remember a now divorced wife or husband, we remember what happened in order to imaginatively fit with who we believe we are now. In the same way, in remembering a major work-related episode, say a business acquisition that we had led that may not have delivered the value it had promised, it is likely to undergo a subtle reinterpretation, inserting some information and dropping some other information so that our beliefs about our own capability remain intact.

In the workplace our recollection of events can become influenced by our beliefs about our role in the organisation and how we wish to be seen by others. Therefore a leader may imaginatively reinterpret how he/she is valued according to how they wish to be perceived and is genuinely surprised when told that the organisation no longer needs their services. In fact following such an event an individual can often reinterpret why things happened as they did by believing that they made the first move because it was time for a new challenge or they were making plans to leave anyway. That is to say we post rationalise our recall of events in order to confirm our beliefs and internal narratives.

We regularly and selectively glue and paste past experiences into a memory of events in order to support our notion of self-worth or belief in ourselves.

THE IMPACT OF TIMING AND SEQUENCING ON RECALL

The timing and sequence of events also biases our memories, especially the recency of events as we will see. In a series of events you are required to sit through, for example presentations or interviews, the *primacy effect* is the influence that the first stimulus that you saw had on you. At the same time the *recency effect* relates to the influence the last stimulus that you saw had on you. In different situations the primacy of a stimulus (commonly referred to as first impressions) may be more important than the recency effect and vise versa. And although the effects appear symmetrically opposing, the research shows that they occur because of different reasons, and that their implications can differ drastically.

While these may seem like simple quirks of memory, they can have a significant impact on decision making. It appears that they have different types of impact influenced by whether the information presented to the decision makers is simple or complex, and if the duration is long or short. Additionally the impact differs if the decision-making process is an end-of-sequence decision or a step-by-step decision. That is to say the impact varies according to whether we are presented with a large amount of complex information quickly and we do not have time to make step-by-step evaluations and we withhold our judgement/decision to the end as contrasted with a decision maker making evaluations incrementally, developing a view progressively which builds on each anchored judgement. In that latter case, the most recent information we are provided with seems to take a greater prominence.

However research shows that when faced with a long session of interviews or presentations, whether or not we make evaluations as we go, the primacy effect is more likely to play out as we become mentally tired and simply rely on our first impressions of a given candidate or presenter and these take prominence.

As a Private Equity (PE) investor attending a day-long and complex Management Presentation given by the key executives in the target entity, unless there is a process of making judgments along the way, it is likely that the last presentation will have a lasting (positive or negative) impact. Clearly this could colour the judgements being made about the target entity and its players and could materially influence the approach you decide to take when moving to the due diligence stage and the alertness and vigilance with which you do so.

Close Up

We present two real case scenarios, both of which demonstrate the impact of memory on decision making. For obvious reasons these scenarios, while keeping close to the accuracy of the circumstances, have details changed in order to protect confidentiality.

CASE 1

Peter left the meeting confident he had finally secured the sign-off for the implementation strategy for what was probably the most critical investment decision the company had made in decades. It had been a tough, long and tedious debate but Peter was pleased he had got the agreement of the executive group on the implementation plan and was relieved that the US$150 million IT infrastructure spend was finally getting the attention it deserved as an important transformation. It represented the single largest infrastructure spend the company had ever made. The CEO was clear that while this project was a risky decision, if he was not able to deliver the promised cost and revenue benefits, and in particular if the company's legacy systems issues were not quickly addressed, it would make the company irrelevant in the eyes of its customers. In his mind not making a decision on this was not an option. He was counting on Peter to deliver. He also recognised that a history of bad investments (that had not paid off in Return on Investment (ROI) and deflected the company's focus from critical market issues), had adversely influenced the opinions from the Board down to the market leaders who were far from convinced about this new investment. The CEO realised that Peter was going to have a challenge shifting the mindsets of his peers.

Leading up to this all-day meeting, Peter had experienced many months of 'difficult' conversations with his peers. In particular the market leaders felt that this unprecedented scale of investment had limited their ability to access capital from the Group for growth or for small bolt-on acquisitions in their respective markets. They also regularly brought up stories about similar investments in the past that had failed. Furthermore, in those discussions Peter felt he seemed to be taking one step forward and two steps back, recollections of understandings and agreements evaporating along the way. Despite Peter building a detailed business case, the market leaders felt that Peter had not been convincing enough in the business case for their particular markets. While challenging him about the business case, Peter in turn felt that they were not as prepared to invest the required time to help him scope the potential benefits of the new technology platform for their respective markets in detail, as he hoped they would. Despite this, with the help of the sponsorship from the CEO, Peter secured the data he needed from the divisions, and was finally able to lock in the potential savings number ahead of the Board meeting. The Board meeting to agree the capital expenditure had gone well. Peter had then worked furiously with input from teams reporting to the market leaders on an implementation strategy and plan.

This all-day meeting was to get his peers to sign-off on this implementation plan. During the meeting Peter felt that issues that were covered off before the Board meeting were being reopened and re-litigated multiple times. While the CEO allowed the issues airtime, he was pleased at the end of the meeting that there was agreement on all key aspects of the implementation plan. Peter was not so sure.

Following this meeting and as agreed with the CEO, Peter summarised the key decisions and the agreed next steps, sending the meeting minutes around to all his peers. He was careful in the minutes to ensure he did not overstate the outcomes and kept closely to the sentiment in the meeting and referred to the notes he took of all the decisions made, including reflecting some of the concerns expressed. There were multiple decisions as was to be expected given the complexity of this transformation, including agreeing the delineation of three phases (of the implementation plan) and timings of the start and end dates for each, commencing with the formal appointment of the selected technology partner/vendor. Now relieved, Peter knew he could get the process quickly underway.

Peter first realised there was an issue when he sent out a follow-up note to inform his peers of the appointment of the vendor along with a reminder about the release of promised resources from their respective divisions to the transformation project. John, who led the biggest division, emailed back suggesting that Peter had been premature in appointing the vendor given that the final sign-off had not occurred as yet. Furthermore he suggested that his recollection was that the meeting had agreed the scope of the project following Board approval of the Capex spend, and not necessarily a final signing-off on the implementation plan. In this email John stated that while he understood that appointment of the vendor was one of several next steps, it was a step to be taken only once everyone was in agreement to go ahead with the project as scoped. Once again he reminded Peter of previous investments like this one that have failed to deliver promised benefits and caused major disruptions to the business and to customers.

Peter was stunned and immediately walked into John's office with a copy of the meeting minutes, wondering if they had actually attended the same meeting! How could John have confused the purpose of the meeting as being about project scope rather than implementation plan? What he was most dreading was that the meeting decisions arrived at would be re-litigated in a way that was unconstructive and unproductive in delivering on Board-level expectations, agreements and timing, and wondered if John was in denial.

Peter's decision bias

Peter, who has experienced considerable delays in getting this transformation project underway and waiting anxiously for the 'all systems go' signal, is now faced with a reinterpretation of a meeting outcome he felt was clear all along. His conviction that this was the right thing for the company caused him to not pay as much attention to the obvious hurdles. John, who clearly does not have a high level of emotional attachment to this outcome or to the project per se, has a different recollection of how firm the decisions were, experiencing a big decision gap between scope and implementation. Peter in turn views John's email as somewhat irrational and obstructionist in approach about agreed next steps. After all John knew the Board had signed-off on the project scope. The biases that appear to be operating here largely have their source in the different recollections attached to how firm the decisions had been which in turn is subtlety influenced by differing attached meanings and expectations in the event reconstructions.

What decision might have produced a different, game-changing outcome?

Peter could have better recognised that our memories of events are reconstructed and can be subliminally influenced not only by what we want to remember but also by what suits our own objectives and priorities, the strength of our convictions/beliefs, saliency of outcome, recency of events and so on. A good decision maker in Peter's position (keen to get on with a Board-committed project), would have paid more attention to the process leading up to the final meeting. Given the history of failed investments, Peter would be advised to go back in time and bring greater objectivity to recollections of those failed projects. This could be done by demonstrating how different this one was, ensuring that the market leaders had a more accurate grasp of all the factors that historically drove underperforming investments and extracting objective learning as a way of reframing this new programme of investment. Peter could also have invested more time to understand his own as well as the biases of the market leaders. Peter could engage his peers in a collective process to surface all of their fears and anxieties (also voicing his own), giving everyone a chance to describe their 'worst nightmare' in detail and then working collectively through a risk mitigation plan for each one of those detailed 'nightmares'. Additionally Peter could have managed the conclusion of that final meeting differently in order to guard against selective listening and therefore selective recall. By taking the time to run through all of the key decisions at the end of the meeting and the consequences of those decisions (rather than rely on a record of meeting minutes after the event), conflicting or dissonant views would have had a chance to be aired and explored and had more of a chance of being resolved. Recognising not only his/her own attachment to a particular outcome (as with the attachment of others to a different outcome), it should not have come as a surprise that each had a different recollection of what was agreed. High stakes decision meetings like this one ought to follow a 'tighter' process in order to prevent biased recollections of proceedings or past failed projects that create unnecessary noise in the system.

CASE 2

Acme executives, Sally and Bill, had enjoyed a close working relationship with Triforce, one of Acme biggest clients. They were preparing for the annual client planning meeting with Triforce's COO John and had met earlier to agree the approach for that meeting.

Acme had had a history spanning several decades with this client and despite having lived through several Triforce CEOs and economic cycles, Acme had continued to enjoy a strong relationship underpinned by shared values of innovation and sector leadership. Acme had not sought to exploit this loyalty and both Sally (as Marketing Director) and Bill (as Sales Director) had worked hard to keep abreast with the competitive pressures that Triforce had experienced over the years. Because of the importance of this client, Sally and Bill had kept in close contact with members of their teams to ensure that

Triforce's customer experience on the ground where it mattered was exemplary and given the priority it deserved.

Following the Global Financial Crisis (GFC) however things had changed and there was an increased focus within Triforce's executive team on its strategic options and a major internal strategic review was underway.

At the annual client planning meeting with John, Triforce's COO, sales and marketing performance in each of its markets over the past year was reviewed and forecasts for the following year were discussed. John reiterated that he continued to value the Acme relationship, as did his CEO. He said in particular he valued its continuing reputation of being an innovative leader in the sector and this had proven to be a strong driver for continuing to invest in the Acme relationship and in particular the extension of the Acme contractual relationship for another three years. There proceeded to be a lengthy discussion on sales revenue projections and a debate and agreement on competitive strategies to deal with a particularly strident new entrant into the market with a different business model. The meeting went well and John again reiterated that he valued the strategic nature of these discussions. During the wrap up John touched on the costs pressure he was feeling in several of its markets and had intimated that Triforce may need to consider making some tradeoffs in the coming years, although John was not specific about these. He indicated that Triforce's own strategic review was now underway and he could not necessarily be more specific about these at this stage.

On return to their offices, Sally and Bill (who both felt the meeting had gone well and to plan) agreed to meet later that week following work by their respective teams. This work would confirm the forecasts provided by John, and based on the projected volumes, would help determine the pricing implications and revenue calculations.

At the meeting a few days later between Sally and Bill it was quickly apparent that they were operating from opposite ends. 'Bill, I can't believe that you have gone down the pricing route when John spent considerable time when we met telling us how much he valued our commitment to innovation, tying their own organisational success to this very point. At that price margin we won't be able to continue to innovate with our products and continue to hold on to our market leadership. Did you not hear John repeatedly say he valued our leadership and innovation? It is going to push us backward to a proposition similar to our competitors who as you know continue to languish in this market. I really don't believe that is what John was intending,' Sally passionately argues. Bill responds that while that was certainly an important message from John, he distinctly heard the message that price had now moved to the number one issue and the possibility that they may make tradeoffs against Acme were real. Bill argued that the market dynamics had changed and that customers like Triforce were going to migrate away from Acme due to cost concerns and pricing. 'We've got to get our costs down so that we can be price competitive,' Bill retorts. While Sally recognised the need to be competitive on price she was convinced that Bill had not picked up on the client's emphasis. To her it was clear that the customer valued Acme's leadership and innovation and that they would stick with Acme provided it continued to innovate and lead. Price was a consideration not a driver she argued.

She wondered how having had a shared view with Bill for so long about Acme's competitive edge with regard to Triforce, that Bill could have made this 360 degree turn after this one meeting and assumed such a different position.

Sally and Bill's decision lenses

Sally focuses on and recalls from the meeting what she regards as important to Triforce. As all memory is a reconstruction, Bill also recalls what is salient for him. As a sales director measured on profit, pricing undeniably holds the greatest importance for Bill. On hearing the brief reference to pricing at the end of a marathon client planning meeting, Bill focuses on that clue more emphatically than any other clue about Triforce's real priorities. The differences in the relative importance Bill and Sally place on aspects of the same event they both experienced at the same time has its basis in how each have chosen to reconstruct that event. Saliency as well as recency is playing out in this case. The different inferences that Bill and Sally have chosen to make from the client meeting they attended will materially impact the decisions they subsequently show preference for. This is often referred to as criterion bias. Unless they recognise their respective marketing versus sales view of the world and how that may have influenced their respective positions and their (meeting) recollections, and are able to square off their differing inferences and assumptions from the meeting, they are unlikely to make a collectively wise decision. However, while they were in disagreement, together they are potentially ignoring a bigger issue – that Triforce is now a moving target and, both innovation and price appear to be critical to Triforce. Irrespective of Sally and Bill's respective recollections of the meeting and the relative importance they each attach to either issue, they will need to find a collective position to land on in order to respond competitively and retain Triforce as a client.

What decision might have produced a different, game-changing outcome?

When faced with different recollections and the potential limitations of those recollections, it is important to appreciate the value of an 'and' rather than the 'either or' view. There is rarely one undisputed reality, each of us bring our own reality to a set of events. In order to avoid disproportionate importance being attached to the last thing that was raised, shared or discussed by those attending a complex, full agenda meeting, Sally and Bill could have invested more time ahead of the Triforce meeting discussing and agreeing their approach. At such a pre-meeting, a discussion of the individual (functional) filters through which they will each view Triforce's priorities would have been warranted. For example, a marketing person will naturally focus more on brand and value propositions, while a sales person will focus more on sales and sales revenues. Such a pre-meeting discussion might have helped to heighten their awareness and vigilance, guarding against their own selective listening and therefore selective recall. They could have agreed up front on a clear company position (rather than respective functional positions), acknowledging also their different 'world views' and making the necessary adjustments so that meeting proceedings are interpreted in a more balanced way. Additionally, at the meeting with Triforce, proactively anticipating the innovation versus pricing tensions (along with other tensions), framing the right questions for John to generate more explicit guidance on such competing priorities would have been wise. This would make redundant their need to 'fill in the blanks' of their individual or combined meeting recollections and more dangerously 'second guessing' Triforce's needs.

The Red Flags

You will know when memory may be playing its part in biasing decision making when you see the following:

- differing recollections, despite everyone having experienced the same set of events;

- recounting of events by someone who has much to gain or lose from the decision;

- the apparent reinterpretations of meeting outcomes, through selective listening and recall;

- a decision following a meeting that does not bear resemblance to the debate on the issues at that meeting;

- the tendency for post rationalisation following unfavourable events;

- a particular way of framing an event that influences the accuracy of its recall by others;

- there are differences (among panel members) in the way a person, idea or situation is favourably or unfavourably evaluated/viewed at the end of a set of sequenced events, for example, in a series of interviews or presentations;

- someone displaying a totally irrational avoidance of a situation or opportunity that cannot be explained by more obvious facts or the information in a given situation.

Success Strategies

Success strategies we suggest in order to neutralise the inaccuracies of recall or of reconstructed memories include the following:

Rethink the mindset

- Be especially wary of memory-based judgments, asking where possible to see data or information on which the judgment is based.

- Recognise the filter of 'pain' and how we react emotionally to events that are associated with memory of failure, setback and hardship-related experience.

- Challenge your recall of a prior event to ensure it is not being swayed by how you wish to be seen/perceived or by your self-concept.

- Consider all emotive associations, explicit or implicit, that may be influencing how you or others' recall a given event or series of events.

- Challenge how neutrally you or others may be framing a memory-based decision.

Rethink the players

- Recognise when others are engaging in selective listening (often the source of selective recall) and ensure everyone has given due attention to all relevant issues.

- Regroup with key players if necessary to ensure a shared view of relevant history or of historical events.

- Calibrate – ask what others recall of the event or situation, get as many data points and calibrate those views with yours to ensure a balanced recollection of events.

Rethink the process

- At the end of every meeting, record what was agreed by asking those present 'are we all agreed that this is the decision we have arrived at?'

- Strengthen your meeting summation skills by using this simple 4 point rule:
    1. what have we decided;
    2. why have we decided in this way (to ensure a shared view of rationale);
    3. what are the consequences of the decision;
    4. how will we communicate it outside the room (to ensure one voice).

- Issue simple pre-warnings of the fallibility of memory recall, prior to making the decision.

- When decisions are required following a long series of presentations or interviews, it is best to make evaluations and judgments progressively, rather than suspend judgments till the end.

Notes

1 Memory Faults and Fixes, E. F. Loftus, *Issues in Science and Technology*, 2002.
   Publication of National Academies of Science.
2 Make Believe Memories, E. F. Loftus, *American Psychologist*, Nov 2003.

4

Experience Can Trap

Challenging the myth that the more experience we have the better our decisions.

Every new invention starts with dissatisfaction with what already exists; and what exists is often steeped in experience that can trap us within a narrow band of possibilities. There are few better examples of this than James Dyson, and his inventiveness. So how did one man transform a market previously dominated by appliance giants like Electrolux and Hoover and where basic design principles had remained unchanged for nearly a century?

Five years and 5,127 prototypes later, having been turned down by all the big appliance manufacturers, James Dyson launched the Dyson DC01 – the world's first bagless vacuum cleaner. The G Force Dual Cyclone arrived and revolutionised the vacuum cleaner market. Perhaps in turning down his offer, industry incumbents may have wanted to protect the half a billion dollar sales they secure each year from selling bags! In any case they appear to have been unable to step out of their traditional way of thinking about the household appliance. Dyson has since created a US$1.6 billion business. His ideas were pattern breaking.

It all started one day in 1978, Dyson stumbled across the idea while renovating his house in the Cotswolds, England. He became frustrated with the way his vacuum cleaner quickly lost suction. It was a design flaw, and yet vacuum cleaners had been made that way for 100 years. As the story goes, Dyson thought about the problem, built thousands of prototypes, and finally came up with a vacuum cleaner that used centrifugal force, rather than a bag, to separate the dirt from the air. Today, Dyson has a 23 per cent share of the world market and nearly 40 per cent of the UK market.

Dyson recognised that the reduction in a vacuum cleaner's suction was not due to the volume of dust in the bag, but to the fact that fine dust particles quickly clog the pores of the bag and block the airflow. Additionally, the air leaving a conventional vacuum cleaner was contaminated by the dirt caught in the bag and left the machine dirtier and smellier than the air in the room. The bags themselves can be a problem both to fit and to obtain. They can also dislodge and tear in the machine. Most consumers had complained about these problems for years but had simply regarded them as problems inherent to vacuum cleaning. Industry incumbents were not listening or responding to these customer concerns or frustrations until Dyson came along.

A prolific pattern breaker, Dyson did not just stop at the bagless vacuum cleaner. He invented the bladeless fan and heater and other household appliances in quick succession. Some argued that if his ideas really worked, the big manufacturers would already have developed it. Indeed in 1999, Hoover tried to imitate the bagless vacuum cleaner, forcing Dyson to the courts to protect his invention, finally winning a victory for patent infringement.

So why was Dyson so successful in transforming the household appliance market – a market that had not seen any change for decades? A primary reason was not just superior engineering design with lightweight and design-heavy products, but his dedication to challenging conventional experience. Despite his 'before its time' inventions being marketed at higher prices, the consumer feels as though they are receiving a brand new, insightful product, leagues ahead of the competition.

'Persevere and don't take "expert" advice,' Dyson says. 'Listening to naysayers won't help you develop your idea. Discover problems with your invention through trial and error, and iron them out with ingenious thinking and academic rigour. Challenging convention and creating something new is how all inventions or businesses begin. Be different.'

His pattern-breaking skills have found him a place in museums. Dyson products are now on display at museums across the world, including the Victoria & Albert Museum in London, the San Francisco Museum of Modern Art, the Georges Pompidou Centre in Paris and the Powerhouse Museum in Sydney – a testimony to how he refused to confine his thinking to current product experience.

Dyson is not unique as a pattern breaker, every industry has Dysons, who refuse to fall victim to the experience bias.

The Challenge

Patterns are hard to break, in particular patterns that we have historically experienced and come to rely on as 'rules of thumb' or heuristics. They simplify our lives in that we rely on them to recognise the symptoms that tell us this is not a common cold, that the storm clouds in the sky means we ought to not leave without the umbrella or the flat sales figures we are looking at means our products are losing their appeal or the softer share market is suggesting that investors are moving to what they see as safer investments.

Chapter 3 looked at our memory and how our recall of reconstructed memories of events can bias our decisions. In this chapter we are making the case for how our experience – what we are exposed to and what we learn from that exposure – can play a crucial biasing role in the decisions we make and in some cases limit and constrain the quality of our thinking. We generally think of experience as being an enabler of good, well thought through decisions. We challenge this assumption.

We are influenced by what has worked for us before. We always want to repeat our successes, even if what we did before may not apply in the current situation. Most of us are lovers of patterns and these patterns become the filters through which we solve our daily challenges.

Many of these filters have their basis in the professional disciplines we were trained in or the expertise we have accumulated. How often have you heard someone being referred to as having a 'bean-counter' approach to looking at the business or an engineer's way of looking at the world? Depending on the professional disciplines and frames we use, it filters the world for us. This is not ordinarily an issue unless we allow a single frame to dominate our thinking which will cause us to perceive the world narrowly and in turn all decisions will end up as narrow. The tendency for a CFO to focus on cost levers of a business, rather than work with the line leaders to drive the top line (revenue lever), or the tendency of a risk manager to focus on why a deal should not be done rather than the ways in which a deal can be done within acceptable risk parameters are but two examples of how our prior training leads us to an almost automatic hardwired response. It will require a conscious effort and broader exposure for either the CFO or risk manager, in this illustration, to unlearn patterns they have developed and consolidated early in their professional career. However it is not just prior training (ways of thinking we have been trained in) that drives patterns. Experience also plays a part.

As a simple illustration, leaders who have only ever worked in mature markets will have developed a familiarity and understanding of business models that are relevant in mature markets. However they may not have developed a deeper understanding of the fundamental differences that exist in emerging markets and how this may impact the relevance of this (mature market) business model. That is to say they see through a mature market lens by dint of their long experience. Implications for the strategies such a Market Leader will pursue would be profoundly different, for example, in wealth management. In mature markets like Europe the strategy of wealth preservation is more relevant and most Private Bankers in that environment have honed their skills in wealth preservation strategies for their clients. If you then transported a Private Banker experienced in that market into an emerging market like Asia (where the emphasis is on wealth creation rather than preservation), they will view the world through this 'expert filter' potentially biasing the decisions they make.

Today's companies are exploiting these 'outsider's' insights in more structured ways. An example of this is Eli Lilly's InnoCentive, a crowd-sourcing website where it posts its thorniest R&D problems for anyone to solve and reap financial reward. It is designed to expand the company's brainpower by tapping into a larger pool of innovators than it could ever employ. What is interesting is that 30–50 per cent of the problems posted on InnoCentive are solved within six months, that is, a pace significantly greater than what they were able to achieve without it. More interesting than the pace is the way this happens. Most problems are solved by experts outside the field, for example, chemistry problems solved by physicists, engineering problems by chemists and so on. This is further evidence of what innovation experts have long believed to be true, that 'outsiders' are best able to think outside the box because they are less constrained by the 'common sense' or dogma within a given professional discipline.

A Closer Look

Let's look more closely at our pattern-making and pattern-breaking skills, as this has a profound impact on the extent to which we are able to avoid being trapped by our past experience

There are effectively two types of cognitive filters that influence our behaviour with patterns:

- our micro-filters;

- our expert filters.

OUR MICRO-FILTERS

Micro-filters operate at a more profound level than expert filters. While expert filters derive from complex bodies of professionally-based knowledge we have accumulated through our working life, micro-filters are linked to our 'base' intelligence – our cognitive raw material so to speak. The more sophisticated expert filters then overlay on our micro-filters to create a complex web of filters that operates in a way the decision maker is mostly unaware of.

Both cognitive filters can influence how we see patterns. For example someone who is logical in their cognitive orientation is likely to focus on the mathematics or logic of an idea being presented to determine how convincing it is. On the other hand someone who is more interpersonally oriented may keenly observe subtle mannerisms and non-verbals in the person presenting the idea to determine the conviction behind the idea.

For a long time, we believed that there were only two types of 'base' intelligences from which all of our intelligent decisions were derived – logical–mathematical and linguistic thinking. However in 1983, Howard Gardner, a Harvard psychologist, introduced us to a more comprehensive theory of intelligence, rejecting the notion that there are only two types.[1] He proposed various specific types of intelligences, rather than seeing intelligence as dominated by a single general ability. His approach defines seven intelligences that are 'base' intelligences, also acknowledging that we may all have one or more dominant types of intelligences. This in turn represents our particular 'micro-filter' through which we see and respond to the world around us:

- Spatial intelligence – the ability to visualise spaces with the mind's eye. A spatial person is good with puzzles and when put in an unfamiliar town where others would be hopelessly lost, they will are quick in working a way out. Artists, designers and architects have this micro-filter highly honed.

- Linguistic intelligence – the skill with words and languages. They are typically good at reading, writing, telling stories, memorising dates and learn foreign languages easily. Careers that best suit this style of micro-filter are authors, orators and story tellers.

- Logical–mathematical intelligence – the skill with logic, reasoning capabilities, recognising abstract patterns, scientific thinking and investigation and the ability to perform complex calculations.

Chess players, research scientists and of course statisticians have this micro-filter highly honed.

- Bodily-kinesthetic intelligence – the skill associated with control of one's bodily movements and includes a sense of timing such as good eyeball coordination along with the ability to train responses to become reflexes – sometimes referred to as great muscle memory, that is, they remember things through their body. Top athletes, pilots, dancers, musicians, actors, surgeons and gamers generally have this micro-filter highly tuned.

- Musical intelligence – skill associated with sensitivity to sounds, rhythms, tones and music. They have good pitch, rhythm, tone, melody and timbre and are able to sing, play musical instruments and compose music easily. Careers that suit those with this intelligence include instrumentalists, singers, conductors, disc jockeys, orators, writers and composers.

- Interpersonal intelligence – skills associated with interaction with others. Those high on this intelligence tend to be extroverts, characterised by their sensitivity to others' moods, feelings, temperaments and motivations, and their ability to win others over, work cooperatively and may be either leaders or followers. Sales personnel, politicians, teachers and social workers tend to show higher levels of this micro-filter.

- Intrapersonal intelligence – the skill relating to introspective and self-reflective capacities, a deep understanding of the self and others' strengths/flaws and skilled in predicting and controlling one's own reactions/emotions. Members of the clergy, psychologists, counsellors and philosophers often show high levels of this.

Each of these seven intelligences in a sense represents a cognitive filter at the most basic of levels similar to a micro-lens giving us a different perspective on the world we see. If two people used different filters, they will interpret the same experience quite differently. While we can see what enormous opportunities this can generate for innovation and creative output especially when we work together on a problem, there is also much scope of miscommunication, misunderstanding and dysfunction.

If used well, these filters can open us up to a world of innovation, and especially when strengthened by expertise (see expert filters below). Judging by the number of accidental everyday inventions the world has seen, these filters have the power to potentially block out transformative ideas. From tea bags and penicillin to post-it notes and Braille, all were accidental straying away from bodies of knowledge and expertise developed over years. More interestingly in many of these examples, it was the end user or customer that discovered the new use the idea could be put to – further evidence that we are still very much trapped in our own cognitive worlds, sometimes requiring an 'external' perspective to remove bias and unlock creativity.

OUR EXPERT FILTER

In addition to the micro-filter which has its roots in the nature of our 'base' cognitive skills or intelligences, there is an additional overlay which has its roots in the experience we accumulate along the way.

When we consider an experience that has some similarities to the situation we are faced with, but with some important differences, it may lead us to not place as much importance on the differences as we may to the similarities, overlooking critical differences. We may consequently choose an action most similar to our past experience. We can see how easily this can bias one's perspective and lead to poor judgement.

However it is not only a function of adequacy or extensiveness of experience (or our professional training for that matter) that can cause us to make poor judgements. It is also about a phenomenon called brain dissonance. If some information or experience creates dissonance, for example two dissonant facts that create incompatibility with the accumulated experience in our minds, we invent an explanation to explain away that dissonance and typically will accept one over the other. In the book *Think Again*, authors S. Finkelstein, J. Whitehead and A. Campbell[2] profiled the now well-documented example of Sir Clive Thompson the CEO of one of the most successful UK listed companies, the pest control business Rentokil, who had built a strong reputation over a ten-year period for successfully integrating over 130 small acquisitions. This spate of success was prior to the Securiguard (which was equal to about 30 per cent of the size of Rentokil) and BET acquisitions (similar in size) when he made the fatal (unconscious) error of assuming that it would be very much like all the other small bolt-on acquisitions he had successfully led and integrated. Under pressure to continue to deliver the 20 per cent annual profit increases over the previous decade, he was convinced that small add-on acquisitions simply could not do this. However with these two large acquisitions he overlooked all the red flags that would tell him that the learned pattern of integrating acquisition targets that had worked all those other times no longer made contextual sense.

We all operate with 'expert filters' which are a sum total of our professional training, our specialisation and accumulated knowledge and experience. This in turn influences how we not only define a problem we are faced with but the solutions we most reach for. Whole industries can become trapped by such an experience bias. Typewriter companies declined because they used a single experience frame of typing as their calling instead of using the broader frame of word processing. In contrast Xerox broke out of this experience trap and reframed itself as a document company, not allowing its photocopy experience to define or limit its potential.

However, this expert filter represents not only the type of knowledge but the nature of enquiry we get comfortable with. Both add up to cause cognitive dissonance in the minds of experts. Experts are people that have concentrated their filters in a particular direction/way. The type of knowledge experts accumulate and method of enquiry they predominantly use will often be influenced by the way in which they learnt their specialisation. Someone trained in financial management will have a tendency to focus on aspects of reality that can be quantified. However they may ignore, or at best give superficial treatment to, aspects of reality that are not quantifiable – a case of resolving the cognitive dissonance posed by anything not quantifiable in the mind of this particular expert. In the book *Blink,* Malcolm Gladwell[3] recounts many examples of how experts can miss things because of the expert filters they use. In a world as complex and as volatile as this one, and where as much discontinuous change is occurring, this can have disastrous results on the conclusions experts draw and the decisions they make on the basis of these conclusions. Something James Dyson eloquently points out when he cautions against listening to experts.

As trained professionals we leave our professional training believing in facts, theories and tautologies that form a body of knowledge. It is only later, through becoming more thoughtful about our experiences, so that we extract the right lessons from failure and setback, that some of us develop a level of comfort with cognitive dissonance. When this happens we more readily accept the theory of *it depends*, develop a mature disrespect for any theory and become more comfortable with holding competing or polar opposite ideas in our heads, when making judgements and decisions.

DISCOMFORT WITH PERCEIVED ERRORS

Our discomfort with errors often intensifies as we become more skilled and expert in our field which then has a chilling effect on our creativity in finding new and different solutions. Creative people handle cognitive dissonance (perceived errors in their minds) well, and show genuine curiosity in understanding these perceived errors better, rather than rationalising them away. However at school, at university and then later in our professional life we are taught to worry about errors and learn to not make mistakes. Mistakes are costly, we are told in the organisations we work in, and we learn to be careful, to be controlled and avoid taking too many risks in the decisions we make. However creative people appear to have the opposite predisposition. They experiment freely and engage in 'play'. They take chances with thoughts and ideas even though they know they may lead to failure, and they learn to integrate those errors into their thinking process. They are boundary spanners – spanning the boundaries created by disciplinary, functional and expertise barriers, ending up making more creative decisions.

In summary, when making decisions, individually or even in teams, we are likely to view the world from our own functional or expert filter – a product of what we have been exposed to and learned from. This can result in an executive failing to see past the walls of their respective disciplines, biasing their judgement and ultimately impacting the level of collaboration between silos and limiting organisational creativity and agility.

The psychologist Abraham Maslow once famously said, 'When the only tool you have is a hammer, you tend to treat everything as though it were a nail' – a good summary of how our own experience can blind us.

Close Up

We present two real case scenarios, both of which demonstrate the impact of experience on decision making. For obvious reasons these scenarios, while keeping close to the accuracy of the circumstances, have details changed in order to protect confidentiality.

CASE 1

Christian, regarded as an outstanding private banker in top-tier Private Bank Wealth Inc., had tracked a successful career with the company in Zurich over 20 years with some of Switzerland's highest net worth families. His client management skills were spotted early by a Swiss banking veteran Gustav who took him under his wing, mentoring him over many years, and building his self-confidence. When Gustav retired he advocated for Christian to assume the Ultra High Net Worth (UHNW) segment across Europe. This was a big step up for Christian but he was commercially astute and had developed a reputation internally for great partnering with the product teams and as a consequence delivering exceptional client experience and outcomes. Through the quality of his client work he had developed a formidable reputation with competitors across Europe.

Gustav, who was now a member of the Board, following his retirement, advised the Board that if Christian was to be developed as a potential future CEO of Wealth Inc., he had to have a stint in an emerging market to round off his capability and develop a more global outlook.

After successfully delivering on his UHNW segment role, it was decided by the Board that his best next move was to Asia, based out of Hong Kong. Christian was excited by this new prospect and spent several months in Hong Kong leading up to his appointment. During this time he followed several capable market leaders in order to learn the ropes, assessed the talent on the ground, met with the senior team and visited a number of key clients to determine for himself how satisfied they were with their experience of Wealth Inc.

About six months after Christian took on this new assignment, the Board observed that he was not achieving his Funds Under Management (FUM) targets and put it down to his newness in the market and his needing to settle in. However FUM and profitability continued flat in the following six months in a market that was growing very rapidly. The CEO decided to take a closer look and invited himself to the Asia Strategic Review meeting held in Hong Kong, led by Christian and attended by all Christian's market leaders and the functional heads (who reported via a matrix into Zurich). He also tagged on to this meeting some visits with key clients and potential clients. He was not happy with what he saw or heard.

It became very quickly clear to the CEO that Christian's prior experience was getting in the way of successfully landing the challenges in this region.

The product matrix was not working well in delivering to a different market place. Despite Christian's close and deep relationships with his product partners back in Switzerland, he seemed to have not succeeded in persuading them of the different nature of support he required from them. Furthermore, the CEO observed that his private bankers on the ground seemed disengaged with Christian's approach. Christian himself put this down to a differences in culture rather than differences in market characteristics and experience. Furthermore the CEO, in looking more closely at the numbers, saw that they were not getting a bigger share of the wallet of the clients and FUM was leaching away to competitors. He also sensed some unspoken concerns among potential clients about an inflexible approach to opportunities on the ground.

The CEO recognised that Christian had successfully developed his skills in a mature and stable market where the focus has been largely on the preservation of wealth and where most private bankers inherited their portfolios rather than needing to get out there and sell business. However he also recognised that in an emerging market the client demographic was considerably younger, comprising of self-made millionaires, and wealth was not handed down generationally as it was in Europe. As portfolio management and investing behaviour differed profoundly, the strategies had to be necessarily different. Clients were less interested in wealth preservation strategies and keener on growing their new found wealth exponentially and demonstrated a desire to handle their own investing. Despite being a highly successful executive, Christian's experience frame was causing him to miss many vital clues about the nature of the market he was now in and the adjustments he had to make.

Christian's decision bias

Christian struggled to reorientate his thinking to the new paradigm, influenced heavily by an experience-driven frame of reference, one he had built a successful career on. It was clear that this experience was acting as a filter and influencing at a subliminal level all his business and leadership responses to his new assignment. Challenging the relevance of all of one's past experience is difficult for many executives especially when they have been on a successful track.

What decision might have produced a different, game-changing outcome?

Faced with a similar situation, a good decision maker would have taken a different approach and attitude to the assignment. He would have used the preparatory period/trip not just on scheduled 'meet and greet' visits to key customers and getting to know the team, but would have taken several steps to challenge his own assumptions about how successful business was written in the region. He could have done this by:

- meeting with customers who did not bank with Wealth Inc. to try and understand why not; additionally engaging more deeply with them to understand what will have to change for them to move FUM to Wealth Inc. (reading reports on competitor analysis or market benchmarks will not necessarily give him the deeper insights he needed);

- bringing in a subject matter expert in the wealth management arena in Asia to not only seek new and fresh insight into the market, its opportunities and challenges but also to 'disrupt' his own thinking and the thinking of his team;

- reframing the challenge from being one of getting familiar with this new market to one of identifying all the unique attributes of this market that might distinguish it from the market he came from, getting more comfortable with cognitive dissonance, looking not just at similarities but at differences. Recognising that, 'I don't know what I don't know';

- demonstrating curiosity about approaches that appear on the surface to be similar but are not, leading him to dig deeper to reveal the subtle as well as not so subtle regional differences, for example the cultural differences such as the Chinese gambling instinct which is likely to colour the investment habits of Chinese clients;

- instead of accompanying a market leader on a visit, playing the role of a private banker and doing a cold call (cold calling is something that private bankers in Switzerland almost never need to do).

CASE 2

Ashok, as CEO North Asia, was keen to push forward the plans for investing in Vietnam. However he frequently experienced difficulty in bringing his peers along with his ideas because of the strongly entrenched and sometimes combative product versus market views that often remained unresolved. It was clear to him that Vietnam was an emerging economy already successful in many ways and had been an underinvested geography for Genesis Financial Services Ltd. He also recognised that Genesis had been conservative in pursuing new opportunities and this conservatism had precipitated the resignation of several high-profile talent who left to join companies they saw as more aggressive about growth in the region.

Ashok was well prepared for his peers (especially the product heads) to knock his plans. He got in an expert from Gold Partners to review his plans and make recommendations of their own. He had also engaged the Risk Monitor Institute to provide him with an independent view on country and operational risk. In addition, he asked his own team to get every possible analysis on what Genesis's competitors were doing in Vietnam.

Armed with all this information, he had offline meetings with a couple of the perceived detractors among his peer group. They seemed to not share his appetite for growth into new markets, preferring to stick with markets Genesis already had a strong presence in. However Ashok felt that this time they had ignored a number of compelling reasons for expanding into the Vietnam market. He felt confident that he had a clear business case to get his plan over the line.

While the regional CEO whom Ashok reported to was generally supportive of his plans, he did not have as much influence on the product heads who in this matrix structure reported directly into their global heads in London.

At the meeting, chaired by the regional CEO, Ashok presented a clearly articulated and compelling case for investing in Vietnam, in order to get the endorsement of the group. His product peers argued that there was compelling evidence that the Vietnam market had greater regulatory standards and this would create issues for some of their products by increasing costs. They were also adamant that commitments to that geography were going to be at the expense of already allocated and necessary investments with new product developments urgently required in other more established markets. The meeting descended into a shambles with a product versus markets metaphorical fist fight. Ashok left the meeting with deep foreboding, knowing that the lack of shared view about opportunities in the region could result in such a time-sensitive market opportunity for Genesis being lost forever and its impact or relevance in the region doomed to decline.

Ashok's decision bias

A peer group's inability to think outside their silos and their experience frames has resulted in Genesis turning its back on what appears to be a great opportunity for Genesis to extend its footprint in the region. The singular functional or expert filters operating within a peer group can be at complete odds with the enterprise-wide view and result in suboptimal decisions for the enterprise as a whole. The competition for scarce resources often exacerbates the intensity of such issues.

What decision might have produced a different, game-changing outcome?

In order to bring a team together we have to first understand what pulls it apart. There are two elements to understanding differences – the first is understanding the nature of those differences and the second is understanding the source of those differences. This process of building collective purpose (in a team like this one) is achieved through building collective awareness. This is done by recognising and openly acknowledging mindset differences driven by different micro- and expert filters, which in turn impacts power relationships, access to resources and contribution. The differences in values and unique history of each group can operate as yet another filter. Had more work been done to build collective purpose, for example exposing the group to well-planned opportunities for members of the group to listen and learn from the diverse experiences around the table, a different conversation and outcome may have been reached. This is not dissimilar to what best-in-class organisations in fact do in immersing themselves in their customers' businesses to better understand how to serve them. In addition, the deliberate slowing down of conversations which can be done by powerful facilitator-led questioning, such as 'What do you/your unit care most deeply about?' 'What values are guiding your thinking?' and so on would have revealed the source of the different world views making it much easier to pinpoint the areas of consensus and areas of contention. If well-facilitated, such a conversation about differences would have led to the gradual discovery and uncovering of similarities. Going too quickly in search of similarities is often counterproductive. Investing in opportunities to build deeper understanding of each other's differences and perspectives will ensure better-quality decisions are made for the enterprise as a whole.

Red Flags

You will know when experience may be playing its part in biasing decision making when you see the following:

- the singular pursuit of a strategy without reference to changing context;

- the 'It has always been done this way' response;

- personal feelings of discomfort with dissonant experience, information or knowledge;

- a single frame dominating our thinking, for example opening new stores is the only way to grow our business;

- entrenched peer conflict;

- experts who are unable to think outside their area of expertise or think (laterally) across the value chain;

- a business platform or operating model that has not been subject to review for some time, despite declining revenues or profits;

- unthinking routinised patterns in an organisation that are never challenged;

- the inability for someone to see grey – perceiving the world in a 'black and white' way.

Success Strategies

Success strategies we suggest in order to neutralise the way our past experiences can disproportionately dominate our decision making include the following:

Rethink the mindset

- Reframing – most experience biases can be tackled through reframing tactics. Much depends on how the question is posed – when the same question is framed in two ways (that are objectively equivalent) people choose differently. Poorly framed problems can undermine the best considered decisions; challenge your initial frame; look for distortions caused by the frame.

- Reflect on whether you are allowing a single frame to dominate your thinking and cause you to perceive the world narrowly, causing the resulting decisions to also be narrow.

- If you are an expert, ask yourself what expert filter you are using and the natural tendencies such a filter may bring to the decision-making table.

- Remain cautious about long-held theories and adopt a healthy scepticism of the firmly-held views of experts.

- Develop an ease with dissonant information, paradox and adopt the theory of 'it depends' judiciously.

- Self-reflect: ask yourself deep reflective questions and seek honest answers (from yourself and others):
  - What patterns am I not seeing?
  - What voices am I not listening to?
  - What risks am I not planning for?
  - Get back to the 'why' of the business, rather than the 'how' or 'what' in order to avoid using a limiting experience frame when thinking about organisational purpose.

- Argue against your own position on an issue.

Rethink the players

- Role reversal – take the expert out of their regular environment, for example put a marketing or brand manager in a supermarket for the day, or put a business banker into a retail branch for the day in order for them to experience the broader organisational proposition, derive valuable customer context and open up insights that would ordinarily not emerge in the day to day functioning of their roles.

- Bring in external experts and non-experts including customers to 'shake up' prevailing thinking.

- Engage in open source innovation or customer co-creation processes to break down some of the associative barriers you apply in how you perceive a problem internally; *the customer decides* or the *customer knows best* ought to be more than a slogan, consider making it an operating model.

- Create competing teams that will take opposing positions on an issue in order to surface all the issues in a detached way.

- Initiate reverse mentoring to disrupt the thinking of senior executives.

- Identify people you think are good at 'boundary spanning' and include them in your decision-making processes.

Rethink the process

- Create a regular schedule of customer visits for key decision makers in order to 'walk in the customer's shoes' and experience the proposition from the customer's point of view.

- Create opportunities to 'play' or 'experiment' with ideas especially competing ideas, in an unconstrained or unencumbered way.

- (If you are a team leader) absent yourself from early discussions in order to not sway views too early in the process.

Notes

1 *Multiple Intelligences*, H. Gardner, Basic Books, 1993.
2 *Think Again*, S. Finkelstein, J. Whitehead and A. Campbell, Harvard Business Press, 2008.
3 *Blink – The Power of Thinking without Thinking*, M. Gladwell, Little, Brown and Company (Time Warner Book Group), 2005.

5

Optimism Can Cloud

Challenging the myth that the more confident we are of the outcome, the better our decisions.

In 1955 the then Premier of New South Wales in Australia announced a competition to design and build the new opera house in Sydney's Bennelong Point. Invitations to take part were issued to 230 architects from all over the world. There was euphoria about the build, later hailed as a modern masterpiece. Today it represents an iconic building of its time. Jon Utzon, a Danish architect, and his team were selected. At the time it was projected to cost AU$6 million and be completed by January 1963. Six years seemed to everyone like a reasonable time to construct and finish such a building. Building started almost immediately even though Utzon had still not completed the final designs and major structural issues still remained unresolved. However the government of the day had pushed for work to begin early, fearing that funding, or public opinion, might turn against them. The level of optimism the government demonstrated in failing to recognise the enormous complexity (given the site until then had been zoned as swampland) and size of this sponsored project, larger than anything the government had ever attempted, was almost breathtaking.

It was not long before problems hit the project. Storm water flooding of the building site created unplanned delays. As construction had started before the final drawings were completed, the podium columns were not strong enough for the roof and needed to be rebuilt; this was one of several construction issues By 1966 the budget had ballooned to AU$16 million. Meanwhile the disputes mounted and accusations were public and acrimonious between the architects and the government of the day who were funding the project. Eventually Utzon quit and returned to Denmark causing further delay to the project. The project was finally completed at the cost of AU$102 million in 1973, more than 14 times the original budget.

This is not an isolated issue in the building industry or any other industry for that matter. Suppliers of credit for major projects often expect optimism to bias the estimates they receive.

Optimism is a very human instinct and one that permeates not just business but life decisions. According to Yale psychologist David Anmor, about 80 per cent of the population hold optimistic life expectations. The belief that the future will be much better than the past and present does not dent with age. A study in 2005 found that adults over 60 are just as likely to see the glass half full as young adults. There is also a distinction between the optimism we hold for our personal futures which remain highly resilient over time compared to optimism about say the economy, the crime rate or public services which can nosedive with economic cycles.

The Challenge

While our inherent optimism about a better more well-balanced future can motivate and inspire us on to great deeds and even keep us from mental illness (through reduced stress), it can also result in monumental and costly misjudgements as the Sydney Opera House example shows.

In life as in business, optimism permeates all of our expectations. Despite the high proportion of failed marriages for example, people continue to assume that their marriage is not going to be among the divorce statistics. This was demonstrated by the research undertaken by psychologists Lynn Baker and Robert Emery[1] with graduating law students who were planning to get married. Samuel Johnson, the English writer, put it elegantly when he said of our optimism with regards to remarriage – it is the triumph of hope over experience.

In a corporate context, our optimism causes us to seriously underestimate challenges ahead, thereby assuming the simplest of solutions/answers to challenges we confront. For example if a competitor lowers its pricing, your optimism may lead you to the simple conclusion that it is a desperate act to hold on to market share and they can't possibly make money at this new price. But it may in fact be the case that they have innovated their offering in a way that allows them to lower their costs and therefore price. It could also be that they are dropping their price to generate volume for other higher value parts of their business. Dangerously, this bias can create a whole 'dominant logic' on which we base our poorly judged strategic moves in response to competition.

What deepens the impact of the optimism bias is that we tend to attach low probability to negative events and high probability to positive events. According to learning theory we should learn from negative (and positive) outcomes and correct our expectations. But we often don't learn. Our refusal to learn even at a societal level is evident as far back as the thirteenth century when another credit crunch similar to the 2008 one caused a loss of confidence followed by a sudden refusal to lend money.

Work by the University of Reading between a professor of finance and two medieval historians[2] has uncovered the drama behind surprisingly sophisticated medieval trading involving monks and monarchs as well as bankers. The players then developed innovative practices to smooth the unpredictable and unreliable cash flows experienced by large institutions and governments. Sophisticated financial instruments were used then also and included the use of forward contracts in the wool market between monasteries in England and Italian merchant societies, where cash loans would be repaid in wool, and the provision of pension schemes by religious institutions. However, similar to the 2008 credit crunch, there had been a glut of easy money as merchant societies managed large sums of clerical taxes raised for the Pope, enabling them to lend money to kings and to each other. In the early 1290s, the Pope called in much of his money and the French king levied a huge tax on the Italian merchants in France. The final straw was the unexpected outbreak of war between England and France in 1294, when Edward I called on his bankers to raise the money needed to fund his armies. Unfortunately for all involved money was tied up in loans and trade triggering the 1294 credit crunch.

This thirteenth-century story bears a remarkable resemblance to the events leading to the more recent credit crunch in 2008 and numerous credit crunches in between times. This pattern represents yet another example of optimism repeated every 50 or so years on a massive scale (this time compounded by a globally connected financial world). Despite this clear repeating pattern, most of us, including many distinguished economists who track credit cycles, did not see the most recent crunch coming. Optimism was at play again.

Furthermore organisations are built such that certainty is prized and rewarded and uncertainty and ambiguity is not. It is difficult to imagine an executive proposing a plan that they don't articulate with confidence about their ability to deliver on it. Even where risks are voiced they are generally done in relation to an overall confidence that all risks are known, have been assessed and can be mitigated. It is not difficult to see how all subsequent decisions driven by this plan, once approved, become distorted by our confidence, unless we build in a process of continually calibrating our optimism with evolving market realities.

A Closer Look

Optimism can end badly. The optimism that British Petroleum (BP) displayed about the potential risks associated with their oil well technology, claiming that it was virtually impossible that a major deep sea accident would ever occur, ended badly. This optimism was costly, resulting in the Gulf of Mexico oil rig exploration and spill, killing 11 workers and causing a massive environmental disaster that is costing an estimated US$38 billion.

This kind of optimism shown by experienced executives is not isolated. No problem in judgement and decision making in business today is more prevalent or more catastrophic than overconfidence. But both neuroscience and social science suggest that we are more optimistic than realistic, that is, we maintain optimism even in the face of reality. This causes us to have faith in our decisions even when not warranted.

HARDWIRED FOR OPTIMISM

There is a growing body of scientific evidence pointing to the conclusion that optimism may be hardwired by evolution into the human brain.

Prominent neuroscientist Elizabeth Phelps carried out experiments[3] using a functional magnetic resonance imaging (fMRI) scanner to record brain activity in volunteers as they imagined specific events that might occur to them in the future. Some of the events they were asked to imagine were desirable (a great date or winning a large sum of money), and some were undesirable (losing a wallet, ending a romantic relationship). The MRI scanner reported that their images of sought-after events were richer and more vivid than those of unwanted events.

Additionally, we tend to respond to positive messages more than we do to negative messages. Experiments by cognitive neuroscientist Sara Bengtsson[4] showed that people performed better if they were primed with positive messages before they undertook cognitive tests and those that were primed with negative messages did worse. If we are indeed hardwired for optimism it is especially important for leaders to recognise how our physiology combined with the confidence we derive from experience can let us down badly.

POLLYANNA AND OUR BELIEF IN A JUST WORLD

Another form of optimism is the tendency to look for good in all – people or situations. This tendency is often described as Pollyannaism, named after the 1913 book by Eleanor Porter. Contrary to the character in the book who shows irrepressible optimism and finds good in everything, today the word is used pejoratively and refers to someone whose optimism is excessive to the point of naivety or to someone who refuses the accept the facts of a given situation.

While a naive Pollyanna character is unlikely to be found in business today, commercial naivety is not uncommon. This may manifest itself in the failure to see trouble ahead that others can clearly see or in backing an idea or person others can see is likely to disappoint. Such positive-minded people are not helped by a brain that manipulates their perception of reality and may shield them from the painful truth. In V. S. Ramachandran's book *Phantoms in the Brain, Human Nature and the Architecture of the Mind,*[5] he argues that the left hemisphere of the brain sticks to its view of the world, rejecting dissonant information while the right hemisphere as the challenger, looks for inconsistencies. Someone with a Pollyanna view of the world will experience a tough time processing inconsistent evidence that points to a more cynical view of another's intentions or a more realistic view of a challenging assignment with a high probability of failure.

This view of a just world can have dangerous biasing consequences. A dose of paranoia is wise as the founder of Intel, Andy Grove asserts in his book *Only the Paranoid Survive.*[6]

SELF-FULFILLING EXPECTATIONS

Even when one is no Pollyanna, one's expectations can become self-fulfilling, affecting what happens in the future. This happens because expectations transform the way we perceive the world without altering the reality itself.

This is true not only when forced to choose between two adverse options (such as selecting between two courses of medical treatment) but also when we are selecting between desirable alternatives. Imagine you need to pick between two equally compelling strategies. Making a decision may be a tiring, difficult ordeal, but once you make up your mind, something interesting happens. Suddenly – as is the case for most people – you view the chosen offer as better than you did before and conclude that the other option was not that great after all. According to social psychologist Leon Festinger,[7] we re-evaluate the options post choice to reduce the tension that arises from making a difficult decision between equally desirable options. This is sometimes referred to in literature as confirmation bias. True, sometimes we regret our decisions; our choices can turn out to be disappointing. But on balance, when you make a decision – even if it is a hypothetical choice – you will value it more and expect it to bring you pleasure.

Indeed our unconscious biases don't end when the decision is made. Post decision the confirmation bias kicks in so that when the decision turns out well we attribute it to our contribution/capabilities and when the decision turns out badly/suboptimally we attribute it to external factors (including luck or chance).

One of the problems with this of course is that it prevents us from learning from our decisions – good or bad. This will often manifest in allowing post-mortems to be dominated by the tendency to ignore our part in the failure. It will also often result in a lack of preparedness to consider alternative reasons/ hypothesis for one's success.

THE CHALLENGE OF UNFAMILIAR SITUATIONS

When dealing with unfamiliar challenges or issues we are often overconfident about the judgements we make, causing us to sometimes make irrational decisions with unwanted and sometimes very costly outcomes. Data shows that as high as 60 per cent of mergers and acquisitions fail to deliver the promised value. This points to an optimism with which we make plans, often not facing up to the reality that things can go wrong, very wrong in some cases.

Faced with an unfamiliar problem or challenge, the brain searches for useful experiences that may help solve the problem. If we have had what we perceive as related prior experience with the problem, our brains will connect with what we perceive as relevant and appropriate experiences and this fuels our confidence that we know how to solve the problem. However as we saw in Chapter 4, we may make this judgement about what is useful or relevant experience in wholly erroneous ways. For example we may believe we have seen this exact experience before when we have not (it only looks similar on the surface), or we may believe that this experience is different but only in one to two specific ways and have in fact judged those differences incorrectly. Such prejudgements will lead us to assume a confident stance in dealing with the problem. Additionally our experience, as extensive as it may be at one level, may be narrow at another. As an illustration, in taking on the leadership of a business we may assume that growth is essential because we have worked extensively only with growth strategies or we may assume that the only way to enter a new market is to assume that the company must have 100 per cent control, which may in fact end up being a doomed strategy as many businesses have painfully discovered.

Uncovering all the uncertainties involved in a given decision, determining how other decision makers have dealt with these uncertainties and what objective evidence has been used to support the advocated solution are all critical strategies in dealing with uncertainty. Nevertheless our confidence often gets in the way of such meticulous thinking. The question for us then is, how can we remain hopeful – benefiting from the fruits of optimism – while at the same time guarding ourselves from its pitfalls?

Close Up

We present two real case scenarios, both of which demonstrate the impact of optimism on decision making. For obvious reasons these scenarios, while keeping close to the accuracy of the circumstances, have details changed in order to protect confidentiality.

CASE 1

Tom Kaliros, the COO of Metro bank was excited about stepping up to the challenge the CEO and Board had thrown him. Following the Board offsite it was clear that the Board and CEO were looking to Tom's area to make a significant contribution to the cost to income ratio with the target of bringing it down from 55 per cent to where its peer banks around 45 per cent. This meant ripping US$265 million dollars of costs from his operations area and could only be achieved by outsourcing the entire small business mortgage-processing area.

Metro's retail bank's call centres had been successfully outsourced to Philippines with the promised savings secured two years prior. While recognising that this plan to outsource business mortgage operations would be much more challenging, he was buoyed by the report from the consultants he had retained that this was a 'no brainer'. The sums made sense. The location also made sense. Poona in India was significantly more cost-efficient than Bangalore which had attracted much of the first generation of outsourcing activity. Additionally given India's experience and core competence in 'second generation' outsourcing and its sophisticated technology environment, it seemed like a logical option.

Reflecting Tom's own excitement, there was considerable excitement from his team about the start of this high-profile programme of change. However there were also some cautious voices. The Industrial Relations (IR) Director had flagged with Tom potential issues that the unions may have with the resulting 200 job cuts in the mortgage-processing area as a consequence of the outsourcing. Tom reassured the IR Director that while it may be challenging news for the Union to sell to their members, he was convinced that they would soon come to terms with it as preferable to bigger job cuts that would be inevitable if the cost to income ratio stayed where it was. Nevertheless he agreed to see the Union chief whom he met over lunch. Tom did not raise the issue of this outsourcing plan at the lunch, telling him only that the bank was under immense cost pressures.

The offshoring implementation plan was approved by the Board, the Indian Outsourcer Infogen selected and the savings locked in. Tom was feeling very positive as the plan swung into place and, with consultants in tow, made several trips to India to satisfy himself that all was well with the chosen partner. During these visits he met with the CEO of Infogen, Sanjay Gupta, an impressive Harvard-educated Indian with top-tier consulting experience in New York, and was reassured by his enthusiasm and optimism for the programme. Tom saw Sanjay as bright and certainly someone he could trust to deliver. Additionally Sanjay organised for Tom to meet operations managers of Infogen's other major banking clients at evening drinks. Although this event was more social than Tom would have expected, he was comfortable with this given that the consultants had previously visited a number of similar BPO sites on behalf of the bank.

As a start a team of bright and enthusiastic college-qualified Indian BPO staff arrived onshore under the watchful eye of their Indian supervisor. They sat with the onshore team and learned quickly during the four weeks of this trial. However rumblings appeared in the press about Metro staff, due to be made redundant, having to train the people who were going to take their jobs. To settle down this 'noise' Tom issued a press statement saying that all that Infogen was doing was process mapping. In any case, within the four-week trial period, Tom and his project managers were comfortable about moving to Phase 1.

However, quite early in this initial phase, it became obvious there were gaps in the process and the actual understanding of the work required to be undertaken was limited, evidenced by several potentially serious errors. There errors included releasing US$20 million dollars instead of US$2 million dollars to an existing loan client as an overdraft (apparently a decimal point error). These matters were said to be quickly rectified by Sanjay and Tom was satisfied. Practical issues such as how a double-sided mortgage document could be sent via PDF were glossed over. This appeared to be a direct consequence of the decision taken by Tom to limit the duration of the process-mapping stage (a critical stage in any handover). This was not just driven by his anxiety about mounting bad press but also to meet operational constraints. Training therefore commenced prematurely before the offshore staff could fully understand the process.

To keep a tight control on costs, Tom sent a scaled down onshore team to India to observe the implementation of Phase 1. The changeover did not go as smoothly as hoped. There were some unplanned departures among the trained Indian staff which created instability in the core offshore team. It became apparent that staff turnover was running at 40 per cent rather than the 15 per cent that was used as a working assumption in the transition planning. Some of the team that had trained at the Metro HQ seemed to have been assigned to a different bank, diluting the skill levels intended and promised by Infogen for Phase 1. Onshore staff sent offshore to oversee the process and to train and assist offshore staff, who themselves feared for their own jobs, refused to extend their stay overseas to deal with the mounting skill gap issues. Most of the onshore team returned home leaving the process in a precarious and vulnerable position.

Meanwhile, the unions onshore engaged a national-level stop work which brought a number of CBD teams onshore to a standstill and caused the retail banking head to come down hard on Tom for not having the unions in hand and underplaying the impact of the changes.

Additionally, the onshore processing team was allowed to downsize through attrition as the most qualified and experienced staff found alternative roles in Metro and in other competitor banks. These premature departures exacerbated the mounting skill gaps in the offshore teams. The onshore teams were still handling well over 50 per cent of the work – with a severely depleted and demoralised workforce and ever increasing backlogs

Meanwhile things were not going well in India. Rework rates were huge and the take-up date was extended again and again, frustrating the onshore team members who had been promised a redundancy package and a finish date which was looming fast. On closer examination it became clear that Infogen had experience only in retail mortgage processing, not in business mortgage processing, which represents a greater level of process complexity. The added complexity had been grossly underestimated by Infogen. Additionally the importance of local knowledge, experience and understanding of loan/security issues in the offshore team had been severely underestimated.

By the end of the first year customer satisfaction ratings had plummeted. While business customers are typically unlikely to take their borrowings elsewhere (even when unhappy with the service from a bank) their willingness to refer Metro to associates or friends or take new borrowings from Metro was materially influenced. Market reputation and standing was compromised, with some business customers writing directly to the Board to air their frustrations over simple processing issues.

Tom's decision bias

Tom's optimism and can-do attitude in responding to what was already a tough target to meet was evident. His over-reliance on the retained consultant's evaluation of Infogen's capabilities was additional evidence of optimism as was his failure to add margins of error to his estimate of resourcing levels or skill transfer timelines. Tom was lulled into a sense of confidence by Sanjay's 'pedigree' and this overconfidence could have resulted in his antennae not being as sharp in picking up on the 'glossing over' of important operational detail. His under-estimation of union reaction or the impact of a demoralised onshore team on the process was further evidence of this optimism. The way Tom's team dealt with practical process issues was a mirror reflection of their own optimism and desire to help Tom achieve his cost savings target. This led to cutting corners and had serious ramifications on the integrity and quality of process outcomes.

What decision would have resulted in a different outcome?

To successfully execute an offshoring process of this magnitude, a strong risk management process needed to be installed alongside any plan. It would also have been better to give the task to an operating steering group with an entirely different reporting line to Tom's. An independently run 'traffic light' system tracking tolerance levels for desired results at every critical stage may have alerted Tom and his team to problems well before they occurred. Process mapping, a critical first step in offshoring, should not have been compromised in any way despite pressures on time because of the knock-on effects it could have down the line. Time could also have been spent with banks (not competing in the same markets) to better understand the implementation issues and could have provided useful pre-warnings of potential challenges ahead. The late discovery of turnover rates of 40 per cent could have been surfaced and built into planning assumptions had better due diligence been undertaken.

CASE 2

Silvio Maximo was appointed CEO of Capital Bank, a large diversified British Bank decimated during the Global Financial Crises (GFC) and bailed out by the British Government. Silvio was headhunted from Intermedia Banca on the strength of his reputation for building Intermedia from a small Italian bank into a retail banking powerhouse, now the third largest in Europe. Over the previous decade he had presided over Intermedia's growth largely through the successful acquisitions of small building societies, savings banks, car financing companies and mortgage companies. Intermedia developed a strong expertise in integrating these entities and in quickly realising the value of these acquisitions. Its long consumer banking history and its unique model of highly profitable retail banking services had made it a target for headhunters looking for top retail bankers across Europe.

In taking on the job at Capital Bank, Silvio announced that under his leadership the bank would become a 'simpler, more agile and responsive organisation'. Although there was little if any more detail about his strategic plans, there was intense expectation of his ability to repay government bailout monies and quickly return Capital Bank to profitability. Over the next six months

Silvio hired a number of key executives from Intermedia who had played a key part in Intermedia's phenomenal growth. He set about reorganising the bank's management structure, announcing 15,000 job cuts and raising public condemnation. Morale plummeted quickly as the clumsily executed restructure plan was rolled out. At its interim results the bank declared that it was likely to miss financial targets given the poor state of the economy. More in-depth analysis of the results showed that the investment banking and corporate banking divisions of the bank had stood still in revenue terms, while costs had gone up disproportionately.

It was not long before rumours surfaced in the market of Silvio's lack of understanding of the non-retail banking parts of Capital Bank and disquiet among executives outside the retail banking division. This disquiet was driven by what they perceived as strategy flip flops and in particular the failure to understand the need to continue to invest in product capability in the corporate and investment divisions. Furthermore banking analysts and other commentators observed that Silvio's micro-managing style was not going to be sustainable longer term in a substantially more complex entity, even if it had served him well at Intermedia. Spooked by the surprise resignation of the head of Capital's investment banking division, the market made its views known. Stock in Capital continued to slide while Silvio attempted a second management reshuffle. Many inexperienced bankers were promoted in this second restructure. Performance and morale continued to plummet and there were more high-profile departures. Eighteen months after Silvio had assumed the CEO role, the Board made the decision that Silvio was not able to rise to the challenge of managing a large and complex bank with more than just retail banking operations and went back into the market in search of a replacement that had a deeper understanding of the entire banking value chain.

The Board's decision bias

The Capital Bank Board had taken an optimistic view on Silvio's candidature and his ability to run a full service bank. On the strength of his track record with Intermedia (which was strictly retail banking) and in particular his ability to drive strong profitability in that bank, they assumed that he would be able to do the same for Capital. Silvio himself had underestimated the complexity of running a complex full service bank, applying in large part his winning formula that had succeeded for him at Intermedia (Silvio also succumbing to the experience bias discussed in Chapter 4).

What decision would have resulted in a different outcome?

The Board could have undertaken a greater level of due diligence on Silvio's background, instead of relying on the faith they showed in his banking experience. In particular, when a Board does not have members on it with a strong financial services background they may underestimate the complexities and subtleties associated with different elements/areas of banking. A seasoned headhunter advising the Board could have engaged in a greater level of due diligence in putting Silvio forward. On arrival Silvio, determining that he needed to invest more time in the parts of the bank he was not as familiar with, could have surrounded himself with corporate and investment banking expertise who could have helped him challenge his assumptions and preconceptions. It would have been better to spend his first 90 days meeting all of Capital Bank's institutional and corporate clients and sector experts, listening deeply to better understand the different dynamics, funding constraints, growth challenges, risks and so on (as compared with the retail end of the business). In order to ensure he did not make over confident calls, it was critical that he found a way of challenging all of the profit and growth assumptions he had built his successful career on by finding himself a 'sparring partner' that had a deep understanding of wholesale and non-retail banking.

Red Flags

You will know when optimism may be playing its part in biasing decision making when you see the following:

- a unanimous agreement without much debate;

- forecasts that appear to have considerable upside growth;

- a lack of systematic risk assessment especially of the intangible risks;

- short decision-making timeframes;

- an overemphasis on positive aspects of a merger or acquisition;

- euphoria surrounding a high-profile deal;

- a compromised or hurried due diligence process;

- a dismissive approach to risks with a 'this is different' response.

Success Strategies

Success strategies we suggest in order to neutralise the impact of optimism in clouding our judgement and prudence when making decisions include the following:

Rethink the mindset

- Stop to consider reasons why your judgment may be wrong.

- Before embarking on a chosen path, consider how you might actively seek out disconfirming information or evidence that would prove your chosen path wrong.

- Recognise when your excitement about potential success may be blinding you to the risks.

- Ask yourself what are the main uncertainties involved in the decision – how objective is the evidence in favour of your preferred option?

Rethink the players

- Gather people around you who will wear the 'black hat'[8] and generate opposing positions.

- Appoint someone to take the business case apart and find all the reasons why the case won't stack up.

- Appoint a devil's advocate from within the team, assigning them this role formally so that 'push back' is legitimised and given permission.

- Seek out an expert with a very different view about a project or initiative who will be impartial and invest time understanding their view.

- Find a 'sparring partner', who is happy to challenge you in your thinking.

Rethink the process

- Find three sources of data to provide you the ability to 'triangulate' a complex issue to guard against underestimating complexity.

- Get into the habit of developing non-traditional sources of data including from suppliers, regulators and partners.

- Run a performance calibration session or talent calibration session to even out the likelihood of over-confident calls about who has potential or talent.

- Secure a second opinion before taking action as a final reality check.

- Study similar initiatives that have gone wrong in other companies and investigate case similarities and differences.

- Engage in scenario planning as a way of making sense of uncertainty and complexity.

- Conduct pre-mortems (similar to a post-mortem except in reverse) as a way of imagining that the required decision(s) has been taken and the programme or project executed and completed.

- It is now 2–3 years later and you have sight of all the things that have gone wrong and prepare a risk mitigation plan to deal with those visualised risks.

Notes

1 When Every Relationship is above Average: Perceptions and Expectations of Divorces at the Time of Marriage, L. Baker and R. Emery, *Law and Human Behaviour*, August 1993.
2 The Use of Credit Finance by Medieval Monarchs, Dr A. Bell, Professor C. Brooks and Dr R. Moore, ICMA Centre, University of Reading 2008 (research sponsored by Economic and Social Research Council (ESRC)), paper presented in 2010 at History Society Conference.
3 Neural Perspectives and Emotional Impact on Perceptions, Attention and Memory, D. A. Stanley, E. Ferneyhough and E. A. Phelps, *Handbook of Neuroscience for Behavioural Sciences*, John Wiley & Sons, 2009.

4 Priming for Self Esteem Influences the Monitoring of One's Own Performance, S. Bengtsson, R. Dolan and R Passington, *Social Cognitive and Affective Neuroscience*, Sept 2011.

5 *Phantoms in the Brain, Human Nature and Architecture of the Mind*, V. S. Ramachandran and S. Blakeslee, Fourth Estate Ltd, 1999.

6 *Only the Paranoid Survive*, A. S. Grove, Random House, 1999.

7 *A Theory of Cognitive Dissonance*, L. Festinger, Row, Peterson, 1957; A theory of social comparison processes, *Human Relations*, Volume 7, 117–140.

8 *Six Thinking Hats*, E. de Bono, 1985, 1999.

Fear Can Do More Harm

Challenging the myth that the more we have to lose, the better our decisions.

While the Fukushima nuclear disaster in March 2011 is generally seen as the consequence of a rare natural disaster (a 9.0 magnitude earthquake and subsequent tsunami), a parliamentary report in June 2012 concluded that the accident was manmade in more ways than one, both in the lead up to the accident and the aftermath.

In the days following the disaster, there was no official view about the nature of the risk to the public from radiation contamination. Instead the exclusion zone was progressively moved to a wider and wider radius around the accident zone in the days and weeks following the disaster. Each announcement extending the exclusion zone was not accompanied by a detailed analysis of risks to members of the public, who continued to expose themselves unwittingly to unsafe levels of radiation.

Well before the disaster, in 2008, Tokyo Electricity and Power Company or TEPCO had made a tsunami prediction in a report that was delayed in its submission until four days before the accident. Having made this prediction in 2008 it had failed to take preventative measures for such an eventuality and the regulator went along with this non-action. But once the disaster had occurred why did the players in this story consistently fail to align their communication and action with the severity of the disaster?

It is widely accepted now, and following the independent parliamentary panel, that TEPCO officials and the regulators were not adequately prepared. Neither acted fast enough to prevent the explosions that damaged the reactor buildings, or recognised and then admitted that their efforts to cool the reactors and spent fuel pools with helicopters and water cannons were ineffective.

However it was the Prime Minister, and his apparent procrastination immediately following the accident, that is the matter of our interest here.

The Naoto Kan-led Government was criticised for everything from its management of evacuation measures and disclosure to public communication and clean-up efforts, which foreign governments and crises and disaster experts said were insufficient. So was its monitoring of and disclosure of radioactive materials in the food supply and ocean. The Government declared a nuclear emergency status which was announced not by Kan himself but by Yukio Edano, Chief Cabinet officer in Japan. Japanese Government officials tried to comfort the nation by assuring them that the proper procedures were being undertaken, although not disclosing the actual nature of the contamination risks. They also announced that no radioactive leaks had been detected, something that later proved to be inaccurate. The Government communicated Japanese officials' initial assessments of the accident as Level 4 on the International Nuclear Event Scale (INES) despite the views of other international agencies that it should be higher. Experts say the level was far too slowly and successively raised to 5 and eventually to 7, the maximum scale value, and reflected fear of public condemnation. Shortly after Kan's handpicked advisor for the crisis at Fukushima nuclear power plant – Toshiso Kosako, a radiation specialist at Tokyo University – resigned over the 'impromptu' handling of the crisis. 'The government has belittled laws and taken measures only for the present moment, resulting in delays in bringing the situation under control,' he said.

In an April Yomiuri Shimbun poll, 70 per cent of those who responded said that Kan did not exercise leadership during the crisis, many registering their unhappiness at the Government's handling of both the event and its aftermath. A report in Time magazine summarised the events following the disaster as follows: Kan's decisions, as head of state, immediately after the disaster appeared to show fear that revealing the truth may panic the public and a fear (inappropriately given the magnitude of the disaster) of its impact on the fragile and inexperienced government he presided over. His fear of both losing his grip on his fragile government and public condemnation combined to result in his abject failure to personally own the issues. Had he taken control from day one, demanded accountability from regulators and TEPCO, brought in global experts, signalled that contamination of water was a real possibility, he would have shown the courage called for in such a pivotal time in Japan's history. Instead, after labelling the disaster as Japan's worse crisis since the Second World War, he abruptly receded from public view. One of his few public moves was to call for a national-unity government, but the LDP (Japan's Liberal Democratic Party) predictably snubbed his offer.

Supporters of Kan claim that TEPCO had been used to dealing with the previous government that had been in place over a very long period and deep, trusting relationships had not been built with this new and somewhat fragile coalition. However national catastrophes call for strong, courageous and sometimes authoritative leadership, which in this case was absent. The greater the cries of condemnation, the more visible was Kan's fear of facing up to this most complex of leadership tasks.

The independent parliamentary panel, issuing its report in June 2012, blamed the government, industry collusion (putting self-interest before public safety) and a conformist culture that encouraged too much deference to authority. Whatever the official reasons, fear can paralyse the leader's action and lead to a leadership deficit when no decisions are taken (when one is obviously needed). More critically fear has the impact of making irrelevant concerns, (such as concerns for the fate of his coalition government) become key drivers of the decisions that are eventually made. While there is an important cultural overlay on this complex story, procrastination as a consequence of fear is not just a Japanese phenomenon.

While lack of attention ('I don't sweat the small stuff') and arrogance ('they can't touch me') can often characterise poor disclosure, fear is also a major part of it. Fear of the embarrassment surrounding the initial misdemeanour may blind a person to the right (subsequent) decision and start them down a slippery slope of ever-bigger lies to cover the first misstep. The cover-up is always worse than the crime as the previous CEOs of Boeing (Harry Stonecipher) and HP (Mark Hurd) found to their immense cost. In both these cases fear had taken over and subverted the quality of their judgement.

The Challenge

While the previous chapter considered how optimism and overconfidence can potentially impact the quality of our judgements and decisions, fear can play a similar role. Fear is especially prevalent today in decision-making behaviour when we are faced with complexity we don't often understand, volatility we can no longer track and uncertainty we can no longer predict.

Fear and anxiety are natural emotions we experience. Everyone experiences fear. Fear can act as a wise protector, for example protecting us from rushing into a job, or a conversation, a trip or even a marriage. In fact a certain level of alertness and even paranoia is necessary for business success and for self-preservation, a theme reflected in Intel founder Andy Grove's book *Only the Paranoid Survive*.[1]

However fear, if not managed, can have a devastating impact on our ability to function, overwhelming us, sometimes freezing us into procrastination, indecision and non-action. It can take hold of us and squeeze all the optimism out of us and convince us that our plans are unattainable.

Successful leaders experience fear but have found ways of using it effectively in guiding their thinking and judgements. Their ability to confront and deal with the unknown, along with all the fear that uncertainty brings, is very much part of their decision behaviour. Instead of bemoaning chaos and uncertainty they welcome it as a means of building agility in their organisations and teams.

Fear in most cases also carries a message, sometimes helpful and sometimes not. It can convey critical information about our beliefs, our values, our needs and our relationships to the world around us. An example of this is an employee who observes that an aspect of the company's practice is operating on the wrong side of the law but fails to become a whistleblower because they value their career/income more than upholding ethics. Therefore the way our fear bias works is also steeped in our beliefs and values.

At a personal level we can experience many fears that may influence and bias our decisions, the fear of looking stupid, fear of not knowing all the answers, loss of face, loss of power, loss of support, loss of approval and so on. Often such fears driving our decisions may not be conscious, buried deeply and not recognised as a fear by the individual (with the fear). Buried deeply it may form the basis for a general lack of confidence (although we may not recognise it as so) and this generates a deeply embedded self-limiting narrative. This narrative can influence our decision making in a range of ways, often without our knowing it. We discuss this concept of internal narratives later in this chapter.

At an organisational level, fear can grip an organisation, be it the loss of market share, loss of a guaranteed revenue stream, loss of key customers and so on, sometimes causing it to make suboptimal decisions. But fear in organisations can also be beneficial as it can act as a critical counter-force to complacency, overconfidence, arrogance or hubris which can lead organisations to make dumb decisions. Some fear is also necessary if organisations wish to have a robust approach to the management of risk.

There is clearly good fear and bad fear. The Polaroid story, described later in this chapter, while showing elements of a range of biases in their slow response to market changes, shows how fear and avoidance can kill off a company very quickly. This fear was often masked and rationalised as commitment to an enduring brand and an undaunted courage in the face of competition. We will examine this case more closely later on in this chapter.

Whether at the personal or organisational level, we can only make good judgements if we learn the art of decoding fear. As fear can be real or imagined, decoding fear will surface any irrationality that may be at the base of it. However, decoding fear, the skill described at the end of this chapter under success strategies, is far from easy.

A Closer Look

Fear can be rational or irrational. Irrational fear is entirely emotional, such as the fear of flying, and usually much more difficult to decode. Rational fear on the other hand can usually be explained by reason, logic and inference. For example we may have gone into a client meeting convincing ourselves that we were not prepared to drop the fee but come out of the meeting having dropped the fee because of some perceived fear that we may lose the client if we did not relent on fee/pricing.

Fear is often only noticed when an organisation finds itself at a fork in the road and has the choice between taking the road well travelled and the one less travelled. At this point of the journey, it will often have to confront its fear not only of the change, the unknown, but also of the potential losses (quantifiable or not) and of failure. At this point we may take the more courageous decision or we may find ourselves trapped in a position of fear, unable to innovate, improvise or see our way into a different future.

In organisations today, fear plays out in the nature of decisions we take (usually to limit change, loss or failure) and sometimes sits behind decisions that are not taken. To some extent all fear is about change but can be subtly different and reflect interesting nuances:

- Fear of the unknown/change – uncertainty about the future, especially true of organisations that may be confronted with discontinuous change and no longer able to rely on information about a future that is increasingly unpredictable, resulting in hesitation, procrastination and sometimes the failure to take critical game-changing decisions.

- Fear of failure/being wrong – tied closely to the need for *perfection*, this fear promotes anxiety about not getting things right. It makes sense that the best way to avoid the pain of failing is not to do anything at all. Most successful business owners and entrepreneurs have a list of failed attempts behind them. It is the way they learnt to get it right. The fear of failure can prevent us from seizing opportunities that may transform our businesses.

- Fear of loss – loss is often associated with change and often about letting go of something regarded as valuable. At a personal level this could mean loss of face or control. Less evident but equally devastating can be the loss of known routines or the things that define who we are (like a job title, a position or even a corner office). At an organisational level this fear of loss can refer to market share, credit rating or revenue stream. This kind of fear can also kick in as part of merger or acquisition activity, where there is an underlying fear from the acquired entity about loss of autonomy, privileges or similar.

SELF-LIMITING NARRATIVES

So what happens when we feel trapped by fear? The feeling is driven by a narrative that develops (both the individual as well as the organisational level), often subliminally and unknown to the individual with the fear. This narrative is often disguised as strong rationalisation for taking an alternative decision or for not taking a decision and may be accompanied by post rationalisation following what appears to be a missed business opportunity. These narratives are dangerous as they can often set the scene for promulgating other supporting narratives and may in fact be difficult to actually spot. It can create a self perpetuating narrative such as, 'Because we did that it now makes sense to do this.'

Biasing narratives that rationalise our fears away can appear perfectly sound or even honourable and can go like this:

'I am only trying to protect the players.'

'I don't want to compound the issue.'

'It is not clear what I could achieve by taking this action.'

'S/he is really accountable, not me.'

'I will be proved right in the end.'

'I have a responsibility to protect the innocent.'

'They made me do this.'

Externalising blame is a very common limiting narrative as it 'excuses' our ownership of issues, often legitimising non-action and accords (in our own minds) the external party's unparalleled power over our actions.

Fear about the reaction of analysts who are often driven by short-term shareholder value is very real and can cause companies to make bad decisions through fear of being punished by analysts and shareholders. Often this fear is not recognised at a conscious level and even if recognised, is not openly vocalised but is ever-present at a subterranean level. For example, analysts may suggest that a company's product structure is too complex and the resulting cost structure too high (driving down profits) creating a dilemma for the company. If its products and services are part of an integrated client offering, then simplifying its product structure may not be that simple to execute and may need a longer-term horizon. Innovation and better customer segmentation might in this case be more appropriate choices. The failure to make the right choices about what to sell and what to keep, what to do and what not to do may result in long-lasting damage to the customer franchise which can end up being very costly to its long-term competitiveness and viability. A company gripped by such a dilemma may choose not to take on the analysts because of the presumption that they are unlikely to succeed in selling the longer-term gain story. Instead of attempting to shift market perception they decide in favour of a short-term view. Fear can cause us to make decisions that are the easiest to make, but are suboptimal or even completely wrong. In some cases we fail to take a decision altogether. But it is easier to blame it on the 'analysts who just don't get it' rather than taking decisive action for the longer-term viability of the company – the primary task of every CEO and Board. Rather than walk up to value creating investments, a CEO may opt for cutting back costs to achieve a short-term profitability, even when it is clear it will impact longer-term growth prospects. Cost-cutting, they rationalize, will deliver short-term profit and appease analysts/investors. In May 2009, Paul Polman, the CEO of Unilever, made headlines by stating that Unilever would permanently cease providing analysts quarterly earnings (EPS or earnings per share) guidance. He further underscored his observation of the unhealthy emphasis on short-term results rather than long-term value,suggesting that hedge funds should go elsewhere. The courage he showed in bucking the trend and restoring the focus on longer-term value creation has been replicated since by a number of other companies.

FOOLISH COURAGE

Faced with any high-risk decision, business courage is required. Sometimes however our responses can border on foolish when we single-mindedly rush to action, taking on fights we don't need to take on, adopting a 'win every point' approach or seeing any small compromise as suboptimal and so on. This is a difficult balance for strong leaders to exercise because they tend to see taking action as a sign of strength and conviction.

Our fear of failing can also be masked as courage. Fear of failing may cause an executive to make a bold but foolish decision on behalf of the company just to prove his/her critics wrong. An executive can be unprepared to walk away from a project by using the sunk cost rationale and avoid admitting that the project was a bad decision in the first place. In turn this sunk cost rationale can become the licence to throw good money after bad. Killing the messenger who brings news you wish to not hear is yet another common scenario. A soon-to-depart CEO wishing not to damage her legacy may make a foolish decision not to make an expensive but critical investment in environmentally sustainable technology (dressing up the decision as a balanced one), consequently causing the company to miss vital market timing and dooming the company to a lack lustre future, is another example of foolish courage. In this case fear of damage to an up to now solid legacy is at its heart.

COURAGE IS A SLOW BURN

Most of us visualise courage as quick, decisive, impulsive action. But in fact courageous decision makers demonstrate a special kind of risk taking, learned, developed and honed often over many decades. They show calculated behaviour – they set goals that are challenging but attainable, they carefully consider what is at stake, they use influence deliberately to tip success their way, they weigh risks and consider necessary tradeoffs, consider when to make concessions, when to compromise, when to employ the art of losing the battle in order to win the war and of course they develop contingency plans.

Even when recognising the mix of emotions that accompanies high-pressure high-stakes decisions, the intelligent gambler will not take rash or later to be regretted actions. For the best decision makers, no action is hardly ever something they opt for.

Courage, the antithesis of fear in decision making, caused DuPont to maintain its R&D spending even through the Great Depression, thus inventing nylon, neoprene and other products that would earn billions for decades thereafter. What fearful leaders often do in perilous times is nothing. Worried that any action is risky, they sit still. But they aren't safe. The winners in uncertain times are the bold, and the losers are often the cautious hedgers.

There are none more bold than Corrado Passera, who stands out as one of the very few CEOs in Europe who has taken on a large complex government-owned postal service, notoriously change resistant around the world, and transformed it into a revenue-positive company.

In 1990s, Poste Italiane (the Italian Postal Service), the largest company in Italy, was facing huge financial losses following 50 loss-making years. As a public utility, it was one of Europe's most inefficient companies and was synonymous with long queues at the post offices, not so polite clerks at the help desks and late delivery of mail. However, efforts directed towards financial and operational revival of the company started in 1998 when Corrado Passera took over as the CEO of the company.

This example stands out when contrasted with many postal services around the world that fail to take pre-emptive action to reshape their futures and take control of their destiny. Fear sometimes can cause us to become victims of destiny. The case details the courage that Passera showed, a relative outsider, former McKinsey consultant and previously the MD of Olivetti the Italian computer and office equipment company, setting out to prove the cynics wrong in thinking that this trickiest of transformations could not be done.

Under Passera's direction, Poste Italiane was restructured and relaunched, with a strong rebound in efficiency, new business models and entry into financial services through the creation of BancoPosta. With mail volumes declining, Poste Italiane had to look for new revenues streams and ways to leverage its strong retail network in both urban and rural Italy. Prior to this Poste Italiane offered traditional passbook savings accounts and interest-bearing postal bonds. To leverage their vast network, Passera undertook the diversification strategy, auctioning out many of its products and services through partnerships with third-party companies, such as banks or investment funds, thereby eliminating the need for a full banking license. Deutsche Bank, for example, was the partner for loans and mortgages, while Poste Italiane retained the distributor's margins. He continued to reorganise the core business: restructuring of sorting offices; purchasing equipment for the activities of the new delivery centres; modernising and upgrading post offices; making investments in technology upgrades; and restyling the post offices as retail shops.

Passera described his early days: 'When I got there we had two months worth of cash for salaries, negative net equity and no technology. No one believed in the future. I had to make sure the government was behind us and start investing in people.'

Rather than taking an adversarial approach for the next four years, from 1998 to 2001, Passera chose to work closely with the labour unions to reverse losses, cut costs and improve services. During that time the workforce was cut by around 17,500 jobs. Discussing his attitude to turning around a company such as Poste Italiane, Passera is quoted as citing honesty and openness with all stakeholders as critical saying: 'You must always have two visions, the short-term and long-term. We described the situation very openly to the trade unions. We agreed on the possible targets and we agreed we had to reduce costs. Sometimes restructuring plans are not accepted by unions because the costs are only paid by workers. Shareholders, managers and employees all have to make sacrifices. If you want people to be with you in a period of sacrifice, you must clearly establish what the return will be.'

The combination of innovation, diversification, efficiency and most of all courage laid the foundations for his success. By 2003 Post Italiane was breaking even. In 2005, the company posted revenues of US$20,485.2 million and a profit of US$433.5 million. In recognition of its exemplary turnover, in 2006 the company was placed in the list of Fortune 500 companies for the first time.

Passera's story is unique amidst continuing losses of many postal services around the world. Those reforms continue to fail, most recently yet another strategic plan was unveiled by USPS (United States Postal Service) in April 2012, in order to save it from ruin.

Passera's story contrasts with Kan's story, reflecting two very different approaches to confronting fear.

DEFENSIVE PESSIMISM

Psychologists refer to a rather commonly observed reaction to fear called defensive pessimism. This is when someone fearful of failure or setback sets low expectations for themselves or others. This helps them cope with the anxiety and stress that can accompany the failure to perform. This may even manifest itself in setting up excuses up front for possible failure, creating self-fulfilling prophecies or plain denial of responsibility or ownership for an issue/task.

While irrational over-exuberance is never wise in any decision, in particular in goal setting, defensive pessimism seems like a safer bet. It is more than just a cautionary approach of under-promising and overdelivering, which is a virtue to the valued. This is a case of making a habit of getting accustomed to losing; of being fatalistic and believing that one can do nothing to improve the chances of success. They give up, doing what is necessary to get by, they retire on the job – physically present but mentally absent. Many leaders and managers who have had a long history working for organisations that make an example of failure breed this kind of fearful leader.

In many organisations, the process of setting budgets will often throw up examples of defensive pessimism, what is sometimes called 'low-balling' or 'sand-bagging'. This is where a market leader might use the previous year's attained revenue goals to anchor their decision about where to set this year's revenue goals. They do this in place of taking a fresh look at how the market is travelling, opportunities and threats to revenue, and then take a freshly calibrated view about where to set the goal. Often fear is behind this budget-setting behaviour – fear of failing, fear of looking like an underperformer, fear of jeopardising bonus outcomes and so on. This kind of fear bias can often drive mediocrity in an organisation.

In her book *Confidence* Rosabeth Moss Kanter[2] purports that individual decisions to hedge bets, hoard information or go passive reinforces the decline of systems and companies. She calls this behaviour the timidity of mediocrity. The base instinct that is operating here is fear.

Courage means taking risks, and that becomes much more difficult when the environment itself becomes dramatically riskier, as it is now. That is why recessionary times such as this so violently separate winners from losers.

Both rational or irrational fear can sap our courage to take action. The key to getting comfortable with fear is the identification of the source of this fear which may be obscured from our view.

Close Up

We present two real case scenarios, both of which demonstrate the impact of fear on decision making. For obvious reasons these scenarios, while keeping close to the accuracy of the circumstances, have details changed in order to protect confidentiality.

CASE 1

In the late 1950s, Polaroid invented the SX70 – a fully integrated camera and film, a camera where the chemical-based development of the pictures took place inside the camera. The picture was ready in about 60 seconds. Polaroid, under its inventor Dr Edwin Land, grew to become a hugely successful company with a product that quickly became a household name. By the 1960s and early 1970s, Polaroid held a monopoly in the instant photography market, and its sales accounted for about 20 per cent of the overall market for film and 15 per cent of the US market for cameras. At its peak the company employed 21,000 people.

Polaroid also had almost a cult brand amongst its followers in the 1970s with icons such as Andy Warhol and David Hockney and an army of artistes among its avid fans. These endorsements created a brand that was seen as 'cool and fun' and the thing you took to parties. However this was a double-edged sword in the sense that if you were wanting to take a serious photo then you reached for a 'serious' camera, not the SX70. This stopped the growth of that market, something that few Polaroid executives predicted, nor did they envision how computers might forever change the use of hard-copy film. Most analysts believed that Polaroid would have had a better chance than Kodak (discussed in Chapter 2) in competing in the digital arena. But none of its leaders looked into the culture to identify a spot where digital could co-exist. It was almost as though they did not want to go there. Fear held them back from facing up to rapidly changing market realities.

In fact the culture of leadership at Polaroid was of chemistry with very little respect for hardware – evidence of an experience bias discussed more fully in Chapter 4. In addition there was an underlying fear of what would happen to their jobs if they got into electronics. The sheer profitability of the film sales business created another obstacle to thinking about new business models. When sales began to decline, Polaroid was faced with a dilemma – change or die. As former CEO DiCamillo remembered, 'We knew we needed to change the fan belt, but we couldn't stop the engine. And the reason we couldn't stop the engine was that instant film was the core of the financial model of this company. It drove all the economics – not instant cameras and not hardware or any other product; it was instant film … So we knew that we had to watch the film and its rate of decline or erosion, and we had to replace it with something that was equally profitable or approximately as profitable.' Instant film had gross margins well in excess of 65 per cent. How exactly would they replace that with something close to that kind of profitability? What stood in the way of seeing more clearly and making the right decision was fear about the loss of easy income.

However this was not the first time Polaroid had failed to anticipate major change. It had failed to respond effectively to the rise in the one-hour photo shops a decade earlier. Avoidance of the issues or not wishing to look too hard to locate the issues was deeply embedded – an underlying fear that the golden age of Polaroid was a dream that might just come to an end. The Kodak story described earlier in the book was another example of bad fear (as opposed to good fear) and demonstrated the company's deep fear of losing what it saw as its core business, only to allow that fear to take hold and prevent it from seeing a different reality and allowing a different set of possibilities to emerge. So what makes some companies comfortable and skilled at facing their fears and others not? More specifically how does this fear and avoidance play out in decisions they make?

Many biases were at work here. First, Polaroid leaders believed that customers would always want a hard-copy print. When customers abandoned the print, Polaroid was taken by surprise. The company culture also showed a collective bias against electronics that went back to the influence of Edwin Land who was sceptical about investing in electronics, burying his head in the sand, unwilling to contemplate that a new technology from physics would replace his founded in chemistry. But this in-built technology bias was not as fatal as Polaroid's business model bias.

In October 2001, Polaroid finally filed for bankruptcy, having amassed debts of almost US$1 billion. The company's share value had slipped from US$60 in 1997 to 28 cents in October 2001.

Polaroid's decision bias

Polaroid clung to the business model that had served it well through the 1970s and 1980s as a money-making machine. It failed to recognise that the generation of revenues itself is not a guarantee of sustainability or long-term survival. Its fear of losing this healthy revenue stream was all consuming and evident at every level – technology, revenue and business model. They were fearful of doing anything that would potentially endanger this three-part mix. This fear resulted in a denial and inattention to everything that was happening around it, wishfully and naively thinking that the good times would continue. It also failed to methodically assess the costs associated with not changing with the market, thereby failing to proactively confront its fears about loss of revenue. It had not exercised its choice to extend into new sources of revenue (even if it resulted in taking a short-term revenue hit) in order to reshape its destiny.

What decision might have produced a different, game-changing outcome?

Had Polaroid taken a consumer and market-centred approach to the business, and created enough organisational agility to house new business innovation, it may still be here today. An annual strategic review and risk management approach that asked of itself what it was assuming and what it was not seeing would have generated a different type of internal conversation and challenged its dominant logic. Its deep fear of losing what it saw as its core business resulted in that fear taking hold and preventing it from seeing a different reality and allowing a different set of market and customer possibilities to emerge.

CASE 2

As CFO of Dodge Instruments PLC, Alex did not enjoy the confidence of his peers who ran the three main divisions. This was not because they thought he did not know his stuff. In fact they all felt he was technically strong, with sound and up-to-date knowledge about regulatory and reporting requirements. However his role at Dodge was somewhat more strategic and required taking a position on Dodge's strategic options

Alex's style was one based on trying to be as small a target as possible, so he attracted as little criticism or conflict (which he found difficult to deal with) as possible. He was perceived by his peers as somewhat invisible, tending to use email as the main form of communication with them even when face to face made more sense. He communicated with his peers on a 'needs-to-know' basis. To help him better understand the business, his peers encouraged him to visit the sites and plants, an offer that was not ever taken up because there were always reasons why it was not convenient for him to leave the office. This added to the impression that he was remote and head office-bound.

His passive and reactive style of engaging with the business, especially with P&L leaders, manifested in him saying very little at meetings ('speaks when spoken to') and rarely providing 'in the moment' decisive input. This somewhat guarded, risk-averse nature did not inspire trust with his peers. In fact he seemed decidedly uncomfortable at the executive meetings and indeed saw it as an unnecessary ritual. The thought of having his decisions challenged at these meetings filled him with fear.

Despite this apparent dysfunctional way of engaging with his peers, Alex however had what appeared to be a good working relationship with his superiors. He was perceived to be upwardly focused with matters of Board reporting and worked closely with the finance committee of the Board which met each month. Alex had worked as CFO with the Chair in a previous company, and seemed to enjoy an especially close relationship with the Chair. This was noted and was troubling not only for the CEO but for his peers who wondered if there had been disclosures that had compromised the separation of duties between the governance and executive arms of the company. Although there was no evidence of any compromise on Alex's part, his lack of a relationship with the Executive created, in their minds, an issue of trust.

The relationship continued to deteriorate when Alex seemed to make arbitrary reporting changes without notifying the divisions, most recently making some significant changes to the capital allocations rules without letting the divisional heads know in advance. Instead he notified the finance managers in the divisions but failed to let his peers know directly, fearing that it would create conflict. His peers were understandably furious as it materially impacted on their budget performance. This became the subject of a rather fiery monthly executive meeting, in which they made their feelings known. Alex quietly apologised, without providing explanation for the approach he took, and showed a reasonable level of contrition. Some of his peers noted that making changes without consultation and apologising later appeared to be a pattern for Alex and wondered if this had to do with his inability to deal with change influentially. However this was by no means the only issue causing frustration. Tough calls had to be made about the transformation programme (which fell into his scope of duties) and it appeared as though, in the absence of Alex's leadership on issues, the CEO was making arbitrary decisions relating to the transformation including allocation of costs which only made matters worse.

Alex's 'light-touch' style extended to how he managed his team of functional reports in the business, resulting in them feeling that they were not being kept informed of what was going on or part of a team. Alex's ability to confront performance improvement issues or deal with tough decisions were inadequate and the team felt under-led. Even though his team were matrixed to the business they serviced, he did not undertake joint performance appraisals with the divisional heads (Alex's peers), leaving their reviews largely to the divisional heads even where he differed in view about individual team member's performance. He preferred not to deal with any potential conflict that could arise from those conversations, even though he had clear views about which of his functional reports were performing and which were not. The fear bias drove his style at several levels.

Alex most enjoyed good working relationships with people who were like him, which limited his ability to engage with the diversity of internal customers and in turn impact his influence as a top-tier CFO. Over time the Board, hearing noise, accepted the CEO's view that it was untenable for a CFO to continue without the backing of his peers and he was eventually replaced.

Alex's decision bias

Alex lacked courage, avoiding difficult issues and making himself a small target not just with his peers but with his direct reports. His fear of conflict had become disabling in the discharge of his responsibilities as CFO and impacted his engagement with other leaders in the business. Even though there was no evidence of Alex's breaching the necessary boundaries between Board governance and executive arms of the PLC, his inability to inspire trust in his peers caused issues to be perceived where there were none. His inherent fear of conflict caused his divisional peers to progressively lose confidence in him and as time went on all professional respect they had for him. Rather than being an aberration, his good working relationship with the Chair of the Board and the Finance and Risk Committee of the Board was a reflection of his comfort in doing as he was told. However in the realm of relationships where he had to put a stake in the ground, take risks, push back or influence those who had the same or lesser power than him, he found himself totally out of his depth, fearing the ambiguity, the conflict and the unpredictability of outcome.

What decision might have produced a different, game-changing outcome?

Despite being an introvert, Alex could have changed the outcomes by initially making some small changes to the way he engaged with his peers. For example, he could have started working with them directly on small initiatives and programmes that were uncontentious in order to build some level of rapport and trust with them. He could have made the effort to take them up on their offer of visits to business sites as it would have been an opportunity to build rapport. Rather than retreating from issues, he could have engaged one on one (even if he dreaded the ritual of the executive meetings) on specific issues by openly sharing his own fears with his stakeholders. A mentor (skilled at influence and conflict management), with whom he could talk his fears through and explore tactics to help him build his confidence in dealing with conflict and push back, would have helped considerably. By failing to engage he was compounding the issues and adding more conflict into the mix. While this sounds like a case of an executive not performing to the requirements of his job, fear can be allowed to drive decision-making behaviour in a range of ways including opting for the 'path of least resistance', delegating the big decisions upwards, reluctance to confront disagreement/conflict necessary for a more balanced decision or just letting others make the decisions one needs to make, eventually diluting one's impact as an executive.

Red Flags

You will know when fear may be playing its part in biasing decision making when you see the following:

- 'low-balling' or 'sandbagging' of budgets and targets;

- the justification to continue an initiative because of sunk costs;

- the failure to face up to reality or steeped in denial about the real situation;

- costly steps being taken towards defending a costly outcome;

- risks being overstated (despite evidence that supports a specific level of risk);

- procrastination on important issues;

- rationalisations for the failure to act on important issues;

- the inability to confront difficult conversations;

- the slowness of decision making in a situation requiring urgent action;

- the failure to stand by the courage of one's conviction;

- someone walking away from or avoiding difficult issues or people.

Success Strategies

Success strategies we suggest in order to neutralise the influence of fear or lack of courage when making tough decisions include the following:

Rethink the mindset

- Ask yourself what is the worst thing that can happen and why might that be so bad.

- Recognise rationalisations that are disguised fear narratives and interrogate these self-limiting narratives openly (or with a trusted other).

- Recognise your courage of conviction and give voice to it, even in the face of opposition.

- Learn how to become conflict competent and build the skills required to have tough conversations.

- Think about a time when you succeeded and hold on to that feeling as it can generate the positive energy for change that you need to make (visualisation is a technique that elite sports people use to master their fears about losing/failing).

- When facing high stakes decisions measure your courage against a set of clear non-negotiable values, for example, pride in the company you work for or happy if the deal appears tomorrow in the newspaper headline or showing duty of care to people who work for you or providing meaningful employment or protecting the environment and so on. Using values as a touchstone will help you separate out courage from foolish courage.

- Use this checklist for decoding your personal fears:
  - Name the fear:
    - in order to be able to manage fear, we need to recognize what exactly it is that we fear and name it. Fear can be obscured.
  - Accept that fear is a legitimate/useful response:
    - fear can be useful in that it can prevent us from taking unnecessary risks.
  - Take a reality check:
    - there is no such thing as a risk-free decision; take action on your fears recognising that any misjudgments or mistakes are chances to learn.

> - Reinterpret and reframe your fear:
>   - ○ ask yourself in what ways the fear you experience might be a positive force for change and how it may derail your plans.
> - Seek perspective
>   - ○ consult others who may have been in a similar situation to get their take on the issue and learn from how they may have managed their fears.
> - Unbundle your fears
>   - ○ shrink your fear; recognise that fear can loom larger than justified because of our very human tendency to assume the worst. Take smaller decisions that will allow you to recover/ rebalance more quickly. Go for smaller wins with lower risk and then work your way up to bigger wins.
>   - ○ seek out those that don't hold those fears and understand what filters they may be using.
>   - ○ recognise that you are not alone in your fears and talk to others (extend this group beyond just business) whom you recognise as having mastered their fears productively.

Rethink the players

> - Select into your team those who are willing to voice contrary views and independent opinion.
>
> - Recognise and reward those that speak up.
>
> - Seek out those who don't hold the same fears on a given challenge and understand the filter they may be using.
>
> - Select those who display a courage of conviction and include them in the decision-making process.

Rethink the process

> - When leading a large organisational change where the destructive impact of anxiety (about the change) descends and deflects the attention of teams, try to remove fear by getting the team together and collectively engaging in this process:
>   - ask the team to imagine every bad scenario, even those that are only remotely possible — the 'worst nightmares';

- give everyone a chance to describe those scenarios in detail and then to 'peer into the darkness' together;
- devise a detailed plan for countering each nightmare – in effect, rehearsing the best collective response to each potential issue;
- once fears have surfaced and been dealt with, the team has a protocol in place for every worst possible scenario and a set of next steps to mitigate real or perceived risks and fears, all of which will build team confidence.

Notes

1 *Only the Paranoid Survive*, A. S. Grove, Doubleday (division of Random House), 1999.
2 *Confidence*, R. Moss Kanter, Random House, 2004.

7

Ambition Can Blind

Challenging the myth that the stronger our drive and ambition the better our decisions.

Jean-Marie Messier, the ex CEO of Vivendi Universal, was one of France's most colourful and controversial leaders. The French considered him not French enough (convinced of this not just by his flamboyance and brashness but also by his decision to move to New York into a €20 million apartment paid for by Vivendi); his American business partners saw him as not American enough (in his lack of transparency and openness about underlying performance of the company).

He had a stunning rise, studying in two of France's most prestigious universities; the Ecole Polytechnique and the Ecole National d'Administration (ENA) that even today produce many of France's political elite. He held several roles in the public sector including working in the French Economic Ministry before he joined Lazard Freres, an investment bank, where he stayed for five years before joining the public sector again in 1994. This time he was appointed Head of the French Utility Group Compagnie Generale des Eaux (CGE) – a 150-year-old utility water and sewage company.

Messier's plans for CGE were breathtaking. Within six years he had transformed it into the world's second largest media company (after AOL Time Warner), acquiring Universal Studios and Universal Music among a string of French businesses – TV stations, mobile telcommunications service, theme parks and so on. He renamed his empire Vivendi Universal.

In this process he had thrown all caution to the wind, ignoring all the rules of diversification. His ambition was completely unhinged from the reality of how sustainable businesses are grown. The recession in the early 1990s however exposed the house of cards Messier had built. It exposed the fact that many of his acquisitions had been overpriced and a balance sheet that was over-leveraged with royalties paid for film, music and publishing interests he had acquired totalling US$100 billion.

In March 2002 Vivendi Universal presented a €13.6 billion loss for FY 2001 resulting in a downward revision in the values of its assets. Company shares plummeted, his North American partners lost confidence in Messier and the Board forced him to resign to save Vivendi. But the story did not end there. Rather than going quietly and accepting that he had to pay a price for his incredible hubris, he had to fight one last battle and this related to a €20.6 million golden parachute which he claimed he was entitled to.

This golden parachute had in fact been written into the American part of his contract with Vivendi. However, when the French courts froze this concession immediately, noting that the Board had not actually approved it, the American shareholders joined in with their own class action lawsuit claiming he misled them about the Group's financial health. He tried to also assume control of his New York apartment as part of his severance terms and failed in this bid. He continued to maintain through his defence that nothing that happened to the company was actually his fault.

Hubris and vanity drove Messier to build this business empire. His arrogance prevented him from recognising his ignorance of the media industry. His reckless ambition caused the dilution of value in many of the companies he took over, including that of the Seagram family who owned Universal Studios with whom he merged. Despite advice he failed to pay any serious attention to the complexities associated with integrating diverse business interests in order to extract synergy value. Neither did he seem to have cared about the many careers and jobs he had destroyed along the way.

The Messier story is not unique.

The Challenge

Hubris, a term derived from Greek mythology, denotes arrogance, self-love and excessive pride. In psychology it is often connected to the superiority complex, messiah complex or narcissistic complex and usually signifies the loss of balanced judgement, a career consumed with ambition that is self-centred and not organisation centred.

Ambition is good. It drives people to achieve and to improve themselves. Without ambition, continents would not have been discovered; inventions that have made the world a healthier place would not have been made and businesses would not have been developed. Andy Grove of Intel, Howard Schultz of Starbucks, Michael Dell of Dell Computer Corp are all examples of pioneers who dreamed of a better place and made that ambition a reality. Although we recognise ambition as essential, we also regard it as slightly dangerous. When unchecked it represents hubris. We don't approve of those who abuse ambition, but we don't respect those who lack it.

People who demonstrate extreme ambition tend to display a number of interesting traits, using people for their purpose, cutting corners to get ahead, craving the spotlight, and spending a disproportionate amount of time self-promoting themselves and their achievements. It is then not hard to see how their decisions can become seriously biased.

Niccolo Machiavelli, Italian diplomat, historian and political theorist who lived in early sixteenth-century Italy in a period of considerable turmoil, derived a sophisticated picture of governance and control tinged with immorality and deceit which he described in the seminal work *The Prince*.[1] While it is not known if he condoned this picture, he first advocated what we now call hubris – a high control orientation coupled with a manipulative style. So much so that we now call leaders who show this behaviour Machiavellian.

Hubris can take over a company as well. Dubai World, a diversified international holding company owned by the government of Dubai and Sheikh Mohammed bin Rashid Al Maktoum, operates businesses in property development, hospitality and tourism, retail, aviation and financial services. It owns the world's tallest building, largest shopping mall and an indoor snow skiing resort. It is famed for building the Palms, man-made palm-shaped islands complete with private residences in Dubai.

Then in November 2009, Dubai World announced that it was seeking a delay of at least six months in making payments on its more than US$80 billion in debt which sent the share and currency markets globally into a downward spiral. A week later, company officials re-estimated the problems and adjusted its timetable to 'something longer than six months'.

Investors were not impressed. Moody's downgraded Dubai World, rating much of the company's debt to 'junk' status. For a company whose majority owners include one of the world's richest countries and one of the world's richest men, it was proof that even the world's most prosperous are not immune from the dangers of excess leverage.

Commenting on this debt crisis, Christopher Davidson, an expert in Gulf politics at Durham University in Britain, reported in the NY Times: 'Dubai was fairly much the worst example of overextension. It had the worst debt per capita in the world by far. I would like to put it down as a really enormous white elephant that doesn't have much in common with the regular economy of a regular state.'

He pointed out that this is not the first time overzealous real estate development has wreaked havoc in the area. Only a few hundred miles northwest of Dubai, in what was once called Babylon, Babylonian developers ran into trouble trying to build a tower to heaven more than 2,000 years ago.

There is more to the Dubai story, however, than just a reinforcement to the age-old warning against the dangers of human hubris. There is a lesson here regarding the unregulated relationships between politics, investors and the business community and the failure to challenge decisions. Hubris is more likely to breed when checks and balances are not in place, or where they are in place but do not work to counter biased judgement.

Hubris is generally derived from success. You will rarely see hubris in an individual or an organisation who has not achieved a significant level of success. A career, for example, built on success after success will develop in the individual a feeling of invincibility and a delusion of control, that is, that they are able (by their skill and cleverness) to control everything around them.

Great companies can also become insulated by their own success and lose perspective of what made them successful in the first place. They ignore the warning signs and explain away disconfirming data. Even if they do accept their difficulties, it is explained away as temporary. As the market pressure to perform mounts, they filter out bad data and only present good data (some call this spin), blaming external forces they say they could not have foreseen, and continue to take outsized risks. At this point catastrophic failure is not far behind. The very success of a company can blind it from seeing the cycle of destruction at its door. Destruction can stalk success at the individual level too, like the moth flying too close to the flame causing it to burn its wings. But can those wings be repaired? Yes – sometimes the wings are singed at the edges and recovery is still possible. Sometimes the wings are burnt so severely that recovery is not possible.

A Closer Look

So if hubris is ambition run wild, and often driven by success, let's take a closer look at what is really taking place. What differentiates an executive who responds to success and makes decisions in a more measured way as compared to someone who does not and what has this got to do with decision making? At the heart of it, hubris centres around two delusions. Armed with these delusions or core beliefs it is not hard to see how decisions can become unhinged from the reality facing the leader making the decision.

The two delusions operating here are:

- The delusion of infallibility – the core belief that one is perfect and infallible, not prone to making mistakes. This belief also shows up as a lack of humility which in turn represents the inability (which may once have been shown and then progressively lost) to see that one's success may have been a function of luck or chance. Taken to the extreme this is a belief in one's infallibility.

- The delusion of control – the core belief that one can control everything: people, environment and so on. This belief assumes that everything is predictable and taken to the extreme, the individual believes they are all seeing, all knowing.

PATHOLOGICAL ROOTS

People who stray into the hubris realm often will have carried some of this pathology from their childhood. For example some practitioners in psychiatry maintain that the delusion of infallibility can be traced back to Narcissistic Personality Disorder, a diagnosis that may exist at a very young age. This delusion may be independent of success, presenting with symptoms of a strong sense of entitlement and grandiose sense of achievement regardless of the level of success achieved in reality.

The delusion of control, experts say, can often be traced back to a childhood where the child may have looked to exert control over their troubled world because of a chaotic childhood. Early parental divorce, domestic violence or similar factors can create a chaotic world for a child who then reaches for everything they possibly can to make sense of and exert control over this chaotic world. Whatever the source of these traits, they show up in a number of ways:

- a grandiose sense of self-importance (exaggerated sense of achievements and talents);

- a strong need for admiration driven by one's tendency to overvalue one's self-worth;

- a belief one is special and unique and can be only understood by other special people;

- a tendency to thrive on admiration from others and seek it out;

- a sense of entitlement and expectation of favourable treatment from others;

- exploitative in nature, using people for one's own ends –while consulting others this is often little more than ritualistic;

- preoccupied with ways of retaining that 'specialness' and as a result gets even or takes revenge on people perceived as challenging that 'special' status;

- tendency to categorise others into two camps: you are 'with me' or 'not with me';

- learning little from defeat, becoming masters of self-deception inventing implausible reasons for one's misfortune.

A combination of these traits are evidenced in leaders with overreached ambition.

Psychologists Robert Hogan, Robert Raskin and Dan Fazzini wrote in *The Dark Side of Charisma*[2] that narcissistic leaders typically resist accepting suggestions thinking it will make them appear weak and do not believe that others have anything useful to say to them. These tendencies are easy to spot during the decision-making stage. More importantly, they wrote that they make judgements with much greater confidence than other people and because their judgements are rendered with such conviction, other people tend to believe them. As a consequence narcissists become disproportionately more influential in group situations. The Hollywood characterisation of Gordon Gecko in the movie *Wall Street* was a superbly portrayed example of this kind of hubris-fuelled confidence and biased action.

THE DANGERS OF CELEBRITY

In the business context much has been written about the celebrity CEO. As in the political arena, in the business arena too, we look for a 'wow' leader and show little patience or compassion for a leader who does not show strong charisma and personality. We see as weak leaders who admit mistakes, reveal their vulnerabilities or acknowledge not having all the answers.

A charismatic leader can on occasion be labelled a 'celebrity CEO' because of their perceived attachment to fame and the trappings of fame. They can sometimes end up assuming the responsibility to turnaround a troubled company on a Board's mistaken belief that what troubled companies need is a high-profile, larger-than-life leader, rather than one who is humble and unassuming, and gets on with the job of making the company successful. There are a number of examples of leaders placed in positions of power who lacked humility (the reverse of hubris), ramming decisions through by ego, rather than building coalitions for change, often using their companies to further their own personal brands and celebrity.

This predisposition for us (as followers) to look for the 'wow' factor in our leaders extends to politics as well. Across major economies in the world today there are currently fragile political coalitions in place, working through difficult stakeholder (minority party) relationships stitched together. The voting public however expects instant results rarely showing patience for the investments that fragile coalitions demand in the decision-making process. Political leaders who admit mistakes along the way, rather than seen as strong are perceived as weak. Revealing your vulnerabilities and admitting to your stumbles or flaws is seen as a sign of weakness because it destroys the cult and mystique of your leadership. Politics does not stand alone in experiencing this kind of predicament. We expect our leaders to be more celebrity like. Coupled with the 24-7 news cycle, it is not hard to see how some ambitious leaders can end up paying more attention to their public relations and the personality they wish to project, rather than focusing on delivering results.

As followers, we bring as much bias to our perception of our leaders as the leaders themselves. Until we take a broader, more systems view, of leadership rather than obsessing about personal heroics, our institutions will fail to exercise the checks and balances needed to prevent the rise of leaders like Messier, who fail to serve their companies or stakeholders well and allow this ambition bias to consume and corrupt their thinking.

Close Up

We present two real case scenarios, both of which demonstrate the impact of ambition on decision making. For obvious reasons these scenarios, while keeping close to the accuracy of the circumstances, have details changed in order to protect confidentiality.

CASE 1

In a global wine industry beset by mergers, Southern Horn acquired Lazio Estates wine business, a family-owned company that was 6 per cent the size of Southern Horn in revenue terms and focused at the low end of volume wine. Southern Horn on the other hand had a well-established global reputation for premium wines with three labels dominating the premium end wine sales in the UK and US. Together they represented 50 per cent of the South African (SA) wine industry. This would ordinarily have caused some concern with the country's competition authorities. However those representing the Lazio family in the deal ran the argument that this was a clever defensive ploy to ensure that these iconic wine brands did not fall into foreign hands, appealing of course to the court of public opinion in the midst of the euphoria and fear that accompanies any major industry consolidation.

Both Southern Horn and the Lazio family said at the time that this was a deal that had great strategic fit – Southern Horn extending its product range into the volume end of wine with Lazio Estates extending its reach globally by leveraging Southern Horn's global distribution platform.

Under the deal, Southern Horn agreed a cash for debt deal which gave the Lazio family 13 per cent of the now expanded Southern Horn capital base, two seats on the Board, with the prospect of founder Marius Lazio, now 72, elected as the third later that year. Lazio and his son Simon were directors of Phoenix

Investments which was now, following the deal, a majority shareholder of Southern Horn.

From the start Board governance appeared to be weak, with two of Southern Horn's most senior directors on several exacting global PLC Boards and travelling constantly, which meant that they were overloaded in their other Board duties. On average, these two senior directors attended only 60 per cent of the Board meetings and missed a number of key Board committee meetings, where key governance, risk and people decisions were discussed. One of these two directors was the Chair of the Risk Committee of the Board which held many of its meetings during the period of the deal across bad telephone and mobile connections. The Lazios quickly filled that vacuum, taking control of integration decisions and then bringing in John Siebert (previously CEO and Deputy Chair of Lazio Wine Estates) who was married to Marius Lazio's eldest daughter, further allowing the family to entrench its power base. The Lazios, apart from being cash rich, had no prior experience running a publically listed company and had only ever run a family-owned entity that employed 200 people with only two brands (Southern Horn had 4,000 employees at the time and over 50 wine brands). Governance issues quickly started emerging.

John made many strategic decisions unilaterally which should have gone to the main Board for approval but did not. However his father-in-law, now on the Board, was aware and was involved in most if not all of those decisions. As strong personalities, it appeared that Marius and John were effectively running the company. No one at the time recognised this as a Board governance issue. John quickly installed his chief wine maker from Lazios Estates as Chief Wine Maker of Southern Horn in a company that was more than ten times larger, much more complex in its style and price point of wines. Before long, Lazio's wine makers were in charge in many of the largest of Southern Horn wineries, reversing age-old grape sourcing and viticultural decisions. It was clear that these wine makers only understood low price point and quick-to-market wines. John's focus on higher margin wines resulted in diluting the premium brands which had a smaller margin, flooding the market and slowly destroying Southern Horn's reputation for making premium wines. Some well-loved labels were discontinued much to the disgust of the discerning wine consumer.

John, who had a dictatorial arrogant style, was known to be rude at meetings – treating management team members with disdain and disrespect, especially if they had a contrary view. He did nothing in his early months to learn about the differences between the two entities and, in fact, within days of arriving, openly criticised the management of Southern Horn in public forums. Experienced wine makers were removed when they pushed back on viticulture-related decisions. When growers began complaining about the way they were treated in price negotiations, John was publically quoted as calling them whinging idiots. News gets around quickly in an industry like this one known for its close-knit relationships. Distributors spoke of their disgust in dealing with the somewhat offensive arrogant sales people from Lazio Estates and slowly turned away, giving Southern Horn wines less store prominence and merchandising support. To many it seemed like a reverse takeover as young wine makers from Lazio estates with very little experience were promoted into key wine-making roles precipitating the departure of many wine makers with global reputations who very quickly got winemaker or consultant roles with key competitors. John ran the business on the basis of loyalty and dissent was quickly removed. Those executives who were marketable elsewhere left to join rival wine companies, while those that were not marketable stayed, leaving Southern Horn damaged from this drain on corporate memory. A bullying culture was pervasive through the whole organisation. The Board seemed oblivious to all this.

Shareholder and market analysts were starting to question the big price that Southern Horn had paid and the way in which the integration had gone a year on and, much more worryingly, the failure to extract synergy value. Still the Lazios themselves, including John, remained 'untouched' by this, blaming everything including competition and the oversupply of wine. The Board appeared unable to take any action against the Lazios who were majority shareholders and boardroom rifts started to occur, rumbling on for years, while Southern Horn's reputation as a premium wine company spiralled downwards. Within five years the company had halved its stock value. John in the meantime spent an undisclosed number of millions building a new office for himself in the UK and in SA and continued his bullying behaviour, lavish parties and company-paid holidays. Dissent was crushed and there was no one there to question his decisions. Executive meetings were progressively done away with and questions about transparency of reporting were emerging with rumours that the Lazios had enough support around the Board table now to take the company private, and rid themselves of the scrutiny of shareholders.

Amid continuing market rumours, Institutional Investors forced the Chair to resign. The new Chair said in his first address to the market: 'Southern Horn's problems, in my view, are not to do with wine, winemaking or our basic technologies; they are to do with the way we have been running our business.' A massive write-off of wine inventory and wine assets took place shortly after.

John was forced to resign, just two weeks after the wine-making giant delivered its second earnings downgrade in less than a year. Even after his departure he kept blaming a flood of cheap wines and increased competition.

Four years later Southern Horn was bought by a global beverages company, who embarked on a campaign to increase value and put an end to the deep discounting culture, and brought back a relentless focus on regionality, reversing the Lazio family legacy that had damaged SA's brand in in the wine industry.

The Southern Horn Board's decision bias

While this story centres around the actions of the Lazio family, it is the decisions made by the Board and its implications for Board governance that are of interest here. First the Board allowed the Lazios to play public sentiment about foreign ownership into their hands. This resulted in giving them a larger say than their stake warranted. The poor attendance by the more experienced members of the Board (who had presided over complex deals like this one) resulted in a failure to apply the normal checks and balances of good corporate governance. The failure to challenge decisions allowed the Lazio's hubris to breed unchecked. In particular the lack of due diligence surrounding the appointment of the CEO. Instead the Board allowed the charismatic Lazios to pretty much have a majority say in a matter so vital to Board stewardship. While the Lazios pointed to the experience in the wine industry of Lazio's preferred candidate as CEO, some deeper due diligence may have revealed that the role he had previously played in Lazio Wine Estates was created to fit a son-in-law into a family business, who had no prior experience in running a publically listed company. Issues of experience, capability and merit were also not given sufficient priority in the process. A more vigilant Board may have picked up the clues of things to come, had they judiciously sought an integration plan and used it as a tool to oversee progress and identify major risks proactively.

What decision might have produced a different, game-changing outcome?

In taking on major 'game-changing' acquisitions, the Board needed to ensure that 'all hands are on deck' – all meetings attended by all members of the Board, in particular members with extensive mergers and acquisitions (M&A) experience and expertise. A properly executed global search for a CEO appointed with experience in M&A and in running PLCs should have been a top priority. Issues of experience, capability and merit should have been the only considerations the Board applied in the process of installing a new CEO.

Aclearly articulated transition and integration plan would have ensured that the checks and balances were in place and that progress was accurately reported. The Risk Committee of the Board needed to be active in monitoring not only financial risk, but reputational and operating risk (which in this case eventually destroyed significant shareholder value).

CASE 2

Robert Nardelli became CEO of Home Depot in December 2000, having had no prior retail experience. Using Six Sigma (as he had done when at GE Power Systems), he set out to radically overhaul the company and replace its culture. Almost immediately, he embarked on an aggressive plan to centralize control of America's second-largest retailer after Wal-Mart Stores. He invested more than US$1 billion in new technology, such as self-checkout aisles and inventory management systems that generated reams of data. He declared that he wanted to measure virtually everything that happened at the company and hold executives strictly accountable for meeting their numbers. All this was new to a relatively laid-back organisation known for the independence of its store managers with their folksy, entrepreneurial style. He changed the decentralized management structure, eliminating and consolidating division executives, many of whom were replaced by GE executives who did not have retail expertise. But notably he was criticised for cutting back on knowledgeable full-time employees with experience in the trades and replacing them with part-time help with little relevant trades experience.

Nardelli was keen to take credit for the doubling the sales of the chain and improving its competitive position although this is not entirely accurate. Some of this can be attributed to riding the housing boom in the US. Revenue increased from US$46 billion in 2000 to US$81.5 billion in 2005, an average annual growth rate of 12 per cent, while net earnings after tax rose from US$2.58 billion to US$5.84 billion. Despite his performance, Home Depot stock was essentially steady while competitor Lowe's stock doubled. So why was this performance not translating into the stock price? In fact the stock price remained the same as when Nardelli first arrived six years prior. While not all of the reasons can be attributed to Nardelli's arrogant style and hubris, a considerable part of the lack lustre stock price was because of it.

With the stock price stuck, it did not take long for the many stakeholders he had alienated in the process (employees, customers, market analysts and shareholders) to start venting publically. Among the more muted commentary: Nardelli's 'numbers were quite good,' says Matthew Fassler, an analyst at Goldman Sachs. But 'the fact is that this retail organisation never really embraced his leadership style'. Another: 'He's not a very humble guy. He seems to have enormous energy but needs to be front and center, and that can wear on the Board and the employees after a while,' observed Edward E. Lawler, director of the Center for Effective Organizations at the University of Southern California's Marshall School of Business.

However, among many of Home Depot's 355,000 employees, especially rank-and-file workers, there was little support. They resented the replacement of many thousands of full-time store workers with legions of part-timers, one aspect of a relentless cost-cutting programme Nardelli used to drive gross margins from 30 per cent in 2000 to 33.8 per cent in 2005. Demoralised staff pointed to a 'culture of fear' that was causing customer service to wane.

Possibly more devastating to his chances of a longer reign at Home Depot, Nardelli alienated customers just as thoroughly as he did employees. Staffing cuts led to persistent complaints that there weren't enough workers in Home Depot's cavernous stores to help do-it-yourself customers. In 2005, Home Depot slipped to last among major US retailers in the University of Michigan's annual American Consumer Satisfaction Index. Nardelli dismissed the survey as a sham. 'Bob Nardelli is a smart man, but he doesn't need to be in a high-profile business like retail,' said one former top Home Depot executive. 'He needs to be in manufacturing, a business that does not have such consumer attention.'

Nardelli's relationship with Wall Street analysts was often just as frayed. He openly chafed at their constant focus on some metrics which he publicly dismissed as unimportant or out of date. Credit Suisse First Boston analyst Gary Balter says Nardelli didn't get along well with Wall Street because he was unhappy with analysts' scepticism of the move away from consumer retailing and into servicing professional contractors. 'He blamed a lot of his problems on Wall Street,' says Balter. 'But Wall Street wanted to see results, and they just weren't there.'

The lack of results, at least in terms of an improving stock price, gradually stirred anger among shareholders. Their frustration was exacerbated by Nardelli's large compensation package: more than US$200 million in salary, bonuses, stock options, restricted stock and other perks over the previous six years.

While the Board stood resolutely by him for most of his tenure, questions about his leadership mounted in 2006. Nardelli himself was said to be fed up of years of having to defend his performance record and apologise to shareholders. As a consequence he sought legal opinion on whether the company actually needed to hold an annual meeting. Anticipating that the meeting would be dominated by 'activist shareholders', he was intent on getting it over and done with as quickly and as painlessly as possible. In the 2006 annual general meeting at which no other Board member showed up to a convention centre full of irate shareholders, Nardelli, flanked by two of his executives, led the meeting himself. He gave no presentation on the operations of the company and did not explain the Board's absence and side stepped every question. He famously only allowed shareholders to speak for a minute each, asking only one question each, timed with the digital clock switching off their microphones when their one minute was up! He wrapped the meeting up in 30 minutes. The not so contrite Nardelli explained later, 'We tried a new format. It didn't work.'

In 2006 following the Wall Street Journal's drubbing of Nardelli as the 'poster child of excessive compensation' the Board started reviewing his package. He finally resigned in January 2007 over a final stoush with the Board over his large and controversial package. While he agreed to give up a guarantee that he would continue to receive a minimum AU$3 million bonus each year, he refused to agree to tie the variable part of his compensation to stock price, dismissing the stock price as something a CEO can't control.

Nardelli left to work in private equity-owned companies where he did not have to deal with any annual meetings or shareholder questions.

Nardelli's decision bias

At the end of Nardelli's term with Home Depot in 2007 he had improved profitability substantially. However it was his arrogance and hubris that eventually cost him his job. His acrimonious and very public stoushes with the market and with anyone who criticised him continued until the final standoff with the Board in 2007 showed how divorced he had become from reality.

CNBC named Nardelli as one of the 'Worst American CEOs of All Time'. By the time of his departure he had alienated most of his stakeholders.

What decision might have produced a different, game-changing outcome?

Had Nardelli adopted a more open and consultative approach to the way he led, accepting that there were other ways to improve profitability that did not sacrifice either the customer or the employee, Home Depot may have tracked a different path. This would have required him to become more accessible and listen more deeply given that it was an industry he knew nothing about when he joined. Additionally, to augment his lack of experience in retailing, hiring strong retailers may have helped to challenge some of the assumptions on which Nardelli based his transformation programme. 'Its my way or highway' style of managing led to him terminating many experienced retailers who challenged his views about how to effect the desired change. His approach of categorising those who challenged him as not 'Home Depot material' was an example of his binary thinking and non-inclusive style of management. The Board could also have brought some more objective analysis of his performance earlier in his tenure by comparing Home Depot's rise in revenue and earnings with the rise of the housing boom to track if he was getting ahead of the housing boom wave or just riding it. They could also have taken a broader view of performance, looking at more than profit improvement and questioning how sustainable the growth was.

Red Flags

You will know when hubris or overreached ambition may be playing its part in biasing decision making when you see the following:

- there is very little listening going on – consultation when it occurs is ritualistic;

- dissent being systematically silenced;

- ambition not backed by skill or performance – the prevalence of 'spin' about performance;

- evidence of narcissistic tendencies;

- an attitude or belief that one's actions are infallible (yours and others);

- decisions that appear to be predetermined before decisions are debated;

- a sense of entitlement pervading parts or all of the organization;

- deeply entrenched complacency about one's market superiority or leadership;

- a tendency to assume that success will continue;

- the tendency to dismiss the potential threats from competitors;

- decisions run by a subset of the executive group rather than the whole executive – existence of a powerful 'kitchen cabinet';

- a personality-driven culture – a celebrity CEO admired for their personality rather than their belief in values and value;

- an autocratic, dictatorial style of management;

- a clash of values, for example, business ownership versus family ownership values;

- the dismissing of shareholders' concerns however trivial.

Success Strategies

Success strategies we suggest in order to neutralise the impact of hubris or overreached ambition on decision making include the following:

Rethink the mindset

- Show genuine curiosity in the views of all your stakeholders.

- Treat all stakeholders as having legitimate views and respect their right to provide input even if you don't agree.

- Be curious about what your competitors are doing in order to challenge your own thinking/assumptions.

- Be alert to the fact that success can often be a result of chance or luck, and therefore more transient than you think.

- See dissent as a healthy part of decision making.

Rethink the players

- Surround yourself with people willing to speak truth to power.

- Rely on more than one person or one source of expert advice/input.

- Develop your own process for listening to and engaging with multiple views/stakeholders even if messages are difficult.

- Create an independent Board or Advisory Committee able to vet the decisions made by the executive arm.

- Ensure the external advisors you use are truly independent.

- Get regular 'soundings' on how the company is perceived by all its stakeholders not just some.

- Actively foster minority views as a means of broadening the debate and discussion.

- Reflect on the diversity in the composition/mix of your team and make changes to bring in more diverse thinking and challenge.

Rethink the process

- Build a robust and transparent process for surfacing complaints from the 'coal face' – customers, suppliers and employees and investigate any divergence of view systematically.

- Build a process for closely and reliably tracking and monitoring competitor activity and communicate its implications transparently.

- Ensure all members of the decision-making group are present when key decision are taken.

- When leading a meeting encourage dissent, disagreeable questions or questions that challenge the prevailing view.

Notes

1 *The Prince*, N. Machiavelli, Critical Classics Series, first published 1532.
2 The Dark Side of Charisma, R. Hogan, R. Raskin and D. Fazzini, in *Measures of Leadership*, edited by K. Clark and M. Clark, 1990.

8

Attachment Can Lead Astray

Challenging the myth that the more emotion we have vested in ideas or people the better our decisions.

In 2005, reports first emerged of phone hacking at Rupert Murdoch's media business, News Corporation. It was not until mid-2011, following reports of hacking into the phone of a murdered teenager in Britain that the full extent of Murdoch's troubles began with the launch of a British public inquiry led by Lord Leveson. Up until then, it represented an extraordinary success story about one entrepreneur's vision of becoming a global media force. By 2000 he owned over 800 companies in more than 50 countries with a reported net worth of over US$5 billion, beginning with a small daily in Adelaide, which he took over from his father in 1952 in the south of Australia. However, the phone hacking troubles were the least of the Murdoch-owned News Corporation's worries.

The bigger worry was the culture that Murdoch had created – a culture that had grown up around the ethos of one man who had powerful friends and who believed implicitly that the ends always justified the means. Murdoch' tabloids ran the line that it upheld the value of 'the public has a right to know'. With a strong attachment to this value, Murdoch developed a strong culture where his reporters, desk heads, editors and managing editors also believed completely that they had a right to bring stories to the public's attention and were justified in employing any methods or means to do so. As one of his British paper's editors said in giving evidence to the Leveson inquiry forced on the British Government by an outraged public, he believed then and continued to believe now that hacking into phones to get to the 'truth' of a story was a defensible position.

The continuing inquiry, which started with only one of Murdoch's papers, *News of the World*, has extended its focus to yet another of Murdoch's newspapers, *The Sun*, describing the existence of a 'pay-off culture'. Murdoch had previously insisted that hacking and related misdemeanours were the work of one reporter in one paper. One commissioner of police testifying to the Leveson inquiry said that one reporter at *The Sun* had been given close to half a million pounds sterling over a number of years to pay story sources that ranged from politicians, police to other public officials.

Once attached to such a principle or a way of doing things, it was hard to see how a culture would or even could 'step out of itself' and examine the ethics of its own approaches to doing business. While it was not criminal to acquire a story by any legal means, you can see how easy it is to get swept up by the unswerving attachment to the idea that 'the public had a right to know' whatever the means, allowing it to stray into contentious territory. You would tell yourself that you were protecting the public's interest until of course it crossed the line of what was lawful. Attachment to a way of doing business, a vision, a strategy, a team or an individual can, while unleashing energy and momentum, also lead us seriously astray as it did in this example.

Newscorp is not the only company that has found itself attached to contentious values that permeated how it did business and later proved hard to defend.

The Challenge

Human beings are social beings by nature and attachment, whether to beliefs, principles, causes or to other people, is natural. For instance we often derive our sense of self-worth from others; we derive pride in our work because of the recognition we get from others; we measure our success against the success of others and so on. We explore these tendencies later on in this chapter.

In the workplace, a leader with strong personal attachment to their team will feel a strong sense of loyalty to the team and may be more lenient on issues of performance or behaviour than someone who does not share a similar attachment to the team. However personal attachments can develop not only in relation to people but to ideas or strategies as well as to the emotions that they evoke. This can become a potent combination. In Chapter 4 we showed how the charismatic Sir Clive Thompson, the once CEO of Rentokil, fell victim to the experience bias. He also had a strong attachment to the visceral feeling that accompanied acquisition deals. Describing his experience of close to 130 deals to an assembled audience, he spoke of 'the excitement of the deal process, the early morning meetings, the discussions about bid tactics with investments bankers, the dangers of letting bankers take too much control, the development of argument for the bid documents, the knowledge that the defending company was going through the same process but with probably less experience' and so on. He was hooked not just to the idea of growing by acquisition but was also hooked on the emotion that came with it – a truly dangerous combination that can cloud all judgement.

An organisation can also develop an attachment to strategies and missions that can lead it astray as is evidenced by organisations who continue to hold on to a strategy that was distinctive once and which has run its course. Such attachments can be costly and difficult to break free from and can decimate whole industries. We single out the Swiss watch industry to illustrate how attachment can occur even at an industry level.

Prior to the 1970s, the Swiss watch industry had 50 per cent of the world watch market according to David Landes[1] who wrote *Revolution in Time*. In the late 1950s and early 1960s, Seiko and a consortium of Switzerland's top firms competed to develop the first quartz watch. Seiko unveiled the quartz Astron, the world's first quartz watch in late 1969, while the first Swiss quartz analog watch, the Ebauches SA Beta 21 was launched at the 1970 Basel Fair. Despite these advancements the Swiss hesitated in embracing quartz watches and stayed attached to their national watch industry organised broadly and deeply to foster mechanical watches. By 1978 quartz watches overtook mechanical watches in popularity, plunging the Swiss watch industry into crisis while at the same time strengthening both the Japanese and American watch industries. As the result of the so-called quartz revolution, many once profitable and famous Swiss watch houses became insolvent or disappeared. By 1983, the crisis reached a critical point. The Swiss watch industry, which had 1,600 watchmakers in 1970, had now declined to 600. A research consortium, the Swiss ASUAG group (Société Générale de l'Horlogerie Suisse SA), was formed to save the industry and the result was launched in March 1983 – the Swatch. The Swatch was a huge success. In less than two years, more than 2.5 million Swatches were sold. It took the Swiss watch industry 13 years to overcome the attachment to a technology that had seen its time. There are industries today that are going through similar dislocating change, clinging to debilitating biases.

No industry is experiencing a more visible change than retailing, driven by our behaviour as consumers. Currently, in most countries with broadband access, anything up to 15 per cent of consumer purchases happen on line compared to under 1 per cent just five years ago. Predictions are that this will grow exponentially in the next couple of years and is predicted to be up to 20 per cent by the year 2015 in some countries. Despite this, many high street chains and department stores (long accused of continuing to drag their heels in establishing a functioning online presence) continue to rely almost exclusively on increasing sales through adding more bricks and mortar stores. Beneath these industry-level changes, some companies have more trouble than others coming to terms with change because of their attachments to old business models or platforms.

In Australia, Gerry Harvey, the CEO of Harvey Norman, the largest electrical and appliance retailer with revenues in excess of AU$2 billion, has been very vocal in the media with his complaints about what he sees as unfair competition (from online businesses). Harvey's vocalisations unfortunately fuelled a very public and very ugly conversation with consumers and consumer groups in Australia who see him as being in denial of how the consumer wants to shop. Industry commentators on the other hand have accused him of being asleep on the wheel and of not seeing this rather fundamental change in retailing coming. Harvey instead was devoting his energies trying to convince the Australian federal government to remove the exemption from GST of overseas purchases of less than AU$1,000. His decision to pursue this avenue rather than challenging his own attachment to a historical model of retailing was a failure of judgement. His attachment to the traditional store format also caused him to see online as an enemy of the company, rather than an opportunity. Despite a 30-year history, in the past three years Harvey Norman's stock price has halved. Along with the other major retailers, and after the online furore Harvey created, Harvey Norman somewhat belatedly has started developing a multi-channel strategy, a mixed model, beefing up its online marketing and engagement with social media (fired up by Harvey's complaints about online competitors). With online sales still only representing about 5 per cent of retail sales – albeit growing strongly – annual growth of nearly 20 per cent has been registered in the most recent National Australia Bank's online retail sales index. The major retailers in Australia have been victims to old attachments.

A Closer Look

Decades of assessment work undertaken on interpersonal needs by TalentInvest using the FIRO-B self rater tool (devised by Dr Will Schutz in 1958) provides evidence to support the strength of the attachment bias through the underpinning theory of fundamental interpersonal needs.

NEEDS THEORY

The Schutz theory[2] simply resolves that people need people to satisfy three fundamental interpersonal needs:

- the need for inclusion (the need to belong to something remains the most primal of human need);

- the need for influence;

- the need for connection.

In the situations we encounter day to day, these needs may be met or unmet depending on the proactive action we choose to pursue the satisfaction of those needs. More interesting however is that FIRO-B data from hundreds of test takers shows that we carry preferences around personal relationships (connection) and our belonging to a tribe (inclusion), sometimes at the risk of impact on outcomes (influence). That is to say we tend to gravitate to people who like us or people who are like us, even when it may not further our goals. This raises many important questions. For example is it possible for a professional, such as independent auditors or other accounting professionals to be ever truly independent in the reports they prepare for their clients? We will look at this question later in this chapter.

THE NEED FOR APPROVAL

Our need as humans to have and enjoy emotional attachment is not the problem in itself. It is our need for approval that can often lead us to making bad choices and decisions.

People can unwittingly become addicted to approval-seeking behaviour at an early age. For many of us the need for approval begins in childhood – when we're young, we need the approval of our parents. So we learn to want what they want for us and become good approval seekers. Unfortunately, it can become a problem when we get older and start generalising this approval-seeking behaviour with our teachers, powerful peers and then our bosses.

Somewhere along the line we lose (or never develop) our ability to decide for ourselves what we want. And the habit is set, often for life.

Core to approval seeking behaviour is the presence of holes in our self-esteem which we look to others to fill with their opinions/views and often to confirm that we are worthy. The behaviour can be disguised by our stated desire to have someone understand what we are talking about or going through, or what is important to us about ourselves. But this need for them to understand us better in reality is our need for them to be OK with who and how we are.

Of particular significance here is that those with a high need for approval will make decisions in order to try to prove themselves to others, which may sometimes have disastrous results and is often never the right decision. Apart from proving ourselves, when driven by the need to please others, we are often unwilling to take a stand on anything that may be left field, unpopular or controversial, lest we upset the other party and incur their disapproval, annoyance or anger.

At its root is the 'fear of disapproval' – the fear of what other people might think about you or say about you if you were to really do what you wanted to do and say what you wanted to say and be who you wanted to be. Fear and how fear can bias decisions is explored more deeply in Chapter 6.

To test the extent to which your need for approval or need to please others may bias your decisions, reflect on the following statements:

- When someone disagrees with me I feel upset.

- When someone rejects my idea I feel they think less of me.

- When people like my idea, I feel they like me more.

- When someone challenges my thinking it feels like they are challenging me personally.

- When someone disagrees with my idea I tend to think most others will also disagree.

- I don't feel comfortable disagreeing when the people in the room have more experience than me.

- I give my opinion only when I feel that others will be receptive.

If you find yourself agreeing with most of these statements then your need for approval may potentially bias your decisions. It may be something you could work on with a skilled executive coach and a trusted mentor to build the relevant skills. These skills include learning to say 'no' more often when your needs are being compromised or when someone else's needs hijack your own; defining yourself not by the rules of others but by your own rules; being clear about your value and values and being prepared to put a stake in the ground for those values is critical for sound judgement and great decisions. It is a more evolved stage of adult development according to Robert Kegan who leads this field in his research at Harvard.

BELIEF IN OUR OBJECTIVITY

Concerns about attachments typically arise in the wake of corporate scandals and collapses, and are not confined only to auditors but all professional advisors to corporates.

Research by psychologists shows that when exercising their judgement in making a decision, individuals unconsciously reach conclusions to favour their own interest (or interests of close associates), while maintaining a belief in their own objectivity. Individuals are not knowingly corrupt or unethical. They are simply less objective than they believe themselves to be.

In a recently completed study, Colin Ferguson and Jane Hronsky of the Accounting Department of the University of Melbourne[3] investigated the effects of unconscious bias on professional judgement in a setting where professional and legal standards require independent and unbiased opinions. Their results were interesting.

In their experiment, an independent accounting expert calculates the amount of loss arising from a contract dispute. There were two parties to the dispute, and each party is entitled to retain their own expert to provide valuation evidence. However, in providing this professional opinion, the professional accountant is bound by a code of conduct mandating independence. Their results showed that regardless of this mandate, the judgement is biased towards the interests of the client retainer. That is to say that the loss calculated by the plaintiff's expert witnesses is consistently greater than those of the defendant's expert witnesses.

In another mock-up dispute they experimented with, graduate forensic accounting students, most with professional accounting experience (who had been trained over a 12-week period in the regulations governing expert witness and accountants' independence) were randomly assigned to either the plaintiff or the defendant on a case where liability was not being disputed but where the size of the claim was. Practicing barristers were used to cross-examine each side on their expert reports and their respective opinions on the size of the economic loss. They were randomly assigned as forensic accounting experts to either the plaintiff or the defendant, and required to calculate the economic loss on the basis of identical facts.

They showed that the attachment bias was present in this controlled experiment even in the absence of any real economic attachment to a client, and in the presence of only a hypothetical relationship to a client (plaintiff or defendant). They surmised the effect of attachments to be much greater in the real world, where professionals are paid real money by clients with whom they have a real relationship.

They further observe that in a professional expert opinion case, expectations are strong that professional judgement is not compromised by bias, conflict of interest or the undue influence of others. However, while this is in fact a noble ideal, the reality may be quite different.

All professional service provider relationships are inevitably subject to the attachment bias. Rather than pretending that this bias does not influence expert opinion, it is the responsibility of clients and regulators to take this into account when considering a professional opinion.

In summary, we tend to underestimate the strength of our attachments and their subtle power on our decisions and our contributions. Attachments can have positive consequences but they can also have dire negative consequences and are often not easy to spot. However, while attachments and the need for approval can colour our judgement and decision making, it is our ability to empathise and make emotional connections that makes us human. Emotional intelligence (EQ) – often used as a catch all for such feelings – is necessary for success as a leader. Business literature is littered with examples of leaders who lacked EQ and eventually self-destructed. So how does one strike the right balance? How do we nurture and value our attachments and yet not allow those very attachments to destroy our objectivity? How comfortable are we to stand our ground even when our view may be perceived as unpopular or unpalatable by others, including clients? Strategies in response to these questions are provided later in this chapter.

Close Up

We present two real case scenarios, both of which demonstrate the impact of attachment on decision making. For obvious reasons these scenarios, while keeping close to the accuracy of the circumstances, have details changed in order to protect confidentiality.

CASE 1

Lin, serial entrepreneur and Executive Chairman of Homestar, had always harboured a vision from a young age of becoming China's 'Richard Branson'. He saw the combination of the fastest growing urbanisation in the world and the rapid rise of the middle class in need of more sophisticated household appliances a sure winner. He quickly built a reputation as one of the emerging leaders to watch in Hong Kong business circles, not only for his single-minded drive towards his 'China Vision' but also for his different business approach.

Lin's global outlook had come from his time studying at Yale and subsequently at Harvard where he received his MBA. His time in Harvard had peeked his entrepreneurial instinct while at the same time providing him with the tools with which to turn his entrepreneurial ambition into a concrete roadmap and a sustainable business. On his return to Hong Kong, Lin worked for a number of entrepreneurs building his profile in the local market and using that time to better understand the potential of the Asian marketplace, in particular mainland China, which was starting to outpace growth in any other market in the region.

In 2005 he started Homestar, a household appliance manufacturing company, with backing from Venture Capital and within three years had built it into a strong business with revenues of over US$500 million. In quick succession he built three companies in Hong Kong that manufactured and distributed household products designed specifically for high-density living in Asian cities like Hong Kong. His brand became synonymous with innovative, funky and cool. Everyone wanted a Homestar!

Now he felt ready to capture his prize – manufacturing entry into mainland China. While many Chinese companies were producing for export, Lin believed his strategy of penetrating the domestic market in China was key. He saw a joint venture (JV) with a former state-owned enterprise (SOE) on the mainland called ChongKing Ltd as the way of doing this. The transaction had been made possible through great relationships between Homestar's Hong Kong-based CEO (who reported to Lin) and mainland China government officials. However, one major concession had been requested by the local government – that the R&D function in Hong Kong be included as part of the scope of the JV.

Lin was anxious about this request, seeking counsel from his many global peers who had had experience with mainland China and realised the risks of such a move. However he knew also that while Homestar's R&D capability was its competitive edge, not conceding to this request would limit/delay what he saw as a time-sensitive entry into the China market. Lin's friends advised him against this plan, describing experiences they had had with JVs, pointing out that there were a couple of alternatives he could pursue but which would take time. Lin dismissed them as only 'dipping their toes' in the water and not being decisive enough. Besides he felt that time was critical and continuing to delay his entry into the market would be competitive suicide. He also felt that as ChongKing Ltd was a former SOE, the experience of his peers were not relevant to his situation. His lawyers added their voice of concern also that a 'slowly slowly' approach to mainland manufacturing may be the more prudent approach. Despite all this counsel, Lin quickly put it out of his mind, agreed to this concession in this JV, seeing his 'China Vision' of becoming a household name in China now within his reach.

Lin saw the need for a well-aligned management team and the ability to apply western management methodologies customised to the Chinese context, and put a Homestar core team on the ground consisting exclusively of western-educated Hong Kong Chinese, many of whom Lin had known for many years and trusted implicitly. By inviting two key executives from ChongKing Ltd to sit on his management team, he hoped that he would cement greater cohesion and alignment on the ground. Lin was confident that this JV strategy would deliver his 'China Vision'.

However, the complexity of managing a JV with the involvement of a local government was new to them. Soon after the JV with ChongKing Ltd, local officials pressured Homestar to co-locate R&D activities in China which Lin resisted. However as the local government officials wanted to be involved in all decisions regarding the R&D activities of the company (even though they were still located in Hong Kong), all attempts in product optimisation and innovation were slowed down. When sales started to slow, Lin and his China CEO initiated high-level discussions with ChongKing Ltd and local officials in order to address the perceived bottlenecks to quicker decision making. However, despite repeated discussions, it soon became clear to Lin and his Hong Kong teams that their real influence to effect any change was limited, and that there was no real shared understanding of what the JV terms implied either within ChongKing Ltd or for the local government representatives.

With over 12 months of fruitless negotiations behind them, accompanied by lack lustre sales, Homestar China was being overtaken by several local enterprises that seemed to have a head start, exploiting the troubles that Homestar was experiencing. The more loyal members of his team believing that Lin was now hell bent on throwing good money after bad and fell silent, feeling disempowered by Lin's uncompromising ambition to make this project succeed at all costs. Despite advice from his lawyers to cut loose and terminate the agreement, Lin persevered for another 12 months while he bled all cash reserves built up from profitable sales in other parts of Asia, and watched his 'China Vision' come to nothing.

Lin's decision bias

Lin's deep, long-standing attachment to the 'China Vision' stood unwavering amidst real risks that he seemed to dismiss far too quickly. This attachment seemed to override his sensibilities as a skilled and experienced entrepreneur. He was willing to overlook advice from his most trusted confidantes in the belief that the issues would be resolved by applying 'westernised' notions of how to navigate his relationships on the ground with previous SOE executives and with local provincial officials. His attachment to one way of achieving his 'China Vision' quickly blinded him to investigating and experimenting with more considered alternatives to fast China market entry.

What decision might have produced a different, game-changing outcome?

It is well documented that entrepreneurs can become not only attached but fixated on their vision, optimistically underestimating the obstacles in the way of their success. This contributes to the vast proportion of entrepreneurs who fail. Lin, as an experienced entrepreneur, had no excuse. Standing back and taking another look at his 'China Vision' and exploring alternative means of getting there is an important step that entrepreneurs like Lin have to take. Listening more closely to the voices of experience or voices of caution would have been sensible. More importantly, Lin needed to have developed some real alternatives to getting to the 'China Vision' in two to three different ways and modelled their implications on growth. Lin could have been more cognisant of the view that objections were about the 'how' not the 'what' of his vision for China and shown more emotional detachment to a single way of doing the 'how'. Using a 'if not why not' lens to view each of these alternatives would have made sense. It would also have ensured that his team would not have 'switched off' in the way they did, believing that the decision had already been taken and that nothing they said would make a difference to Lin's unshakeable attachment to how the 'China Vision' could be achieved

CASE 2

Sarah had been heading the construction business within a large conglomerate for many years and had contributed significantly to the growth and expansion of the business she was responsible for. Consequently, she enjoyed a high level of respect amongst her peers and the members of the Board. Together with Antonio, Director of M&A at Gold Partners she had led several successful acquisitions that had delivered great synergy. Over time, the working relationship between Sarah and Antonio had resulted in a deep level of trust. She trusted his judgement which was frequently evidenced in the lead up to and during the due diligence phase of those acquisitions. He had also shown an acute sense of the market, keeping tabs on potential other bidders and on market intelligence on the target entity culture. She felt he showed a great client ethic and integrity in his dealings not just with her but with all parties. As the years went on, Sarah put less and less energy into vetting Antonio's recommendations, while Antonio himself was becoming increasingly self-confident and at the same time more and more aggressive with his deal ideas.

The new deals Antonio was proposing increasingly reflected a higher level of investment and risk. Furthermore, he convinced Sarah that, as a result of the experience gained from all their previous successes, fees for external support and advice could be scaled back with some work being internally sourced within her team and his team. Despite the increasing number of questions and doubts raised by the Risk Committee of the Board regarding the viability and economics of the new deals proposed, Sarah backed Antonio and his plans, without challenging Antonio's assumptions or continually testing the Board's risk appetite.

The Board was puzzled by the increasingly aggressive deals being presented to them. Over time the Board started questioning not only Antonio's judgement in bringing the right deals forward but also Sarah's judgement regarding Antonio. Individual Board members were starting to pick up 'noise' from other external advisors who appeared to be cautioning the Board about the level of prudence being shown in vetting deals. At first a couple of Board members assumed that the noise was motivated by advisors who had lost out to transaction fees they could have earned if they had continued to be involved in providing advice. However it was becoming clear that not all of the noise could be explained away by this.

During the high-profile Phoenix deal, one of the Board members took Sarah aside, sharing with her some of the concerns that were starting to be discussed between Board members. At first Sarah reacted defensively pointing to politically motivated external advisors, but soon realised that this was in fact a widespread although largely unspoken concern that was starting to emerge about her among most of the Board. Sarah felt she had no choice but to reconsider her trust in and reliance on Antonio in order to protect her own reputation with the Board and with the wider market.

She dreaded the meeting she called with Antonio, recognising that it was going to be a difficult meeting for a number of reasons. First it would be a shock to him and the implications for him not only in relation to the Phoenix deal but for Gold Partners. It was also going to be difficult for her as she had enjoyed a deep level of trust in Antonio and in her view he had not let her down – not yet anyway. She agonised if she would tell him the truth or just tell him that the Risk Committee of the Board had decided to institute a new requirement that necessitated the diversification of advisors it used. She felt that this latter reason would perhaps look less personal and perhaps easier for him to accept.

Sarah's decision bias

Sarah allowed her trust in Antonio, his judgement, skill and integrity (as experienced in previous deals) to influence her alertness to the unique circumstances of each subsequent deal. Her over-reliance on one advisor had caused her to be less vigilant to the biases that he would apply to the deals he was likely to be attracted/attached to. Antonio himself, increasingly confident of the company's appetite, was pushing the limits of risk tolerance on behalf of the company.

What decision might have produced a different, game-changing outcome?

By having more than one advisor you can calibrate the quality of advice receive from each source especially when faced with complex deals. Sarah could have taken the role as a more active advocate of the Risk Committee in her dealings with Antonio. Familiarising Antonio more proactively with the risk parameters of the company and in particular making him clearer about the risk tolerance and appetite that were acceptable would have been prudent. This may have headed off any potential confusion. Practising a pre-mortem examination (resembling a post-mortem but in reverse) before every deal is concluded, which is a technique of visualising a time one to two years after the deal was implemented and having sight of all the things that went wrong or not according to plan and then systematically reviewing how each of those issues might have been prevented, would also have been wise.

Additionally Sarah could have utilised other experts to undertake a review of deals once they had been concluded so that a formal independent view could have become part of the mix and contributed to shaping the next deal. This practice would also have kept Antonio more alert to his own attachments.

Red Flags

You will know when attachment may be playing a part in biasing decision making when you see the following:

- reluctance to engage with or explore alternative strategies, even in the face of changes in the competitive landscape;

- advocating for only one way of executing a given strategy;

- a reluctance to take action on poor performing teams/individuals;

- the reluctance to say no for fear it may displease others;

- nepotism and favouritism shown to individuals;

- tribal or parochial behaviour; unquestioning loyalty to an individual or group;

- the employment of a relative into a business either in direct or indirect working relationship with the decision maker;

- the evidence of an overly informal non-work affiliation with the decision maker which can cast doubt on the objectivity of the decision maker;

- the lack of diversity within a team (not just gender) due to the tendency to gravitate to people who are like us or who like us;

- approval-seeking behaviour;

- an expert opinion treated as unbiased; over-reliance on a single source of expert advice;

- the reluctance to challenge business model/strategy in the face of logical reasons to do so;

- the reluctance to review the relevance of a product/service despite market/customer data suggesting a review or rethink.

Success Strategies

Success strategies we suggest in order to neutralise the insidious impact of our attachments on our decisions include the following:

Rethink the mindset

- Recognise when you usually appear to be agreeing with one individual.

- Get into a habit of seeking second opinions.

- Recognise when you may be tribal or parochial in your views.

- Challenge unthinking routines, letting go of 'I have always done it this way'.

- Continually challenge existing paradigms that may have worked/ are working for you as they may quickly become irrelevant.

- Continue to stay vigilant and alert to your over-reliance on advice from a single external source and ensure you are accessing advice that helps you calibrate the sources.

- Consider all the reasons why this strategy may be the wrong one.

- Be alert to personal interests in a given decision and adjust for its impact.

Rethink the players

- Recognise you may have developed an 'inner cabinet' that may be preventing you from getting exposure to other voices that matter.

- Adopt a healthy scepticism about 'expert' advice, accepting that experts could have their own attachments.

- Where you see factions developing, take steps to break them down, encourage partnerships to emerge that ordinarily do not occur.

Rethink the process

- Allow/encourage dissent in team meetings and allow the minority view to emerge so it can be explored more fully.

- Assign someone to take the role of a devil's advocate in order to challenge the prevailing view/proposed strategy.

- Find opportunities to break up natural coalitions, assigning people to tasks on some other basis other than traditional loyalties.

Notes

1 *Revolution in Time: Clocks and the Making of the Modern World*, D. Landes, Harvard University Press, 1983.
2 *FIRO: A Three-Dimensional Theory of Interpersonal Behavior*, Rinehart, 1958.
3 Accountants are Human Too: The Problem of Attachment Bias, *The Conversation*, theconversation.edu.au, September 2011.
In Over Our Heads: The Mental Demands of Modern Life, Robert Kegan, Harvard University Press 1994

9

Values Can Mislead

Challenging the myth that the stronger the corporate culture or underpinning belief system, the better our decisions.

Thabo Mbeki's belief that AIDS was not treatable has gone down in the annals of history as a shameful legacy of his time as a post apartheid President of South Africa (SA) for a decade from 1999. His flawed belief denied his population the treatment they needed which ended up killing so many and continues to impact generations of young people who continue to suffer through loss of their loved ones. According to a paper written by researchers from the Harvard School of Public Health,[1] between 2000 and 2005, more than 330,000 deaths and an estimated 35,000 infant HIV infections in SA occurred 'because of a failure to accept the use of available antiretroviral drugs to prevent and treat HIV/AIDS in a timely manner'.

As Deputy President, Mbeki had acknowledged the seriousness of the epidemic sweeping SA at the 1995 International Conference of People Living with HIV and AIDS. At that time 850,000 people were already known to be HIV positive. In 2000 the Department of Health outlined a five-year plan to combat AIDS, HIV and sexually transmitted infections. A National AIDS Council was established to oversee the implementation of the plan. SA was on a constructive path to dealing with this national challenge.

However, after becoming President, Mbeki changed policy tack and aligned himself with a small group of dissident scientists who claimed that AIDS was not caused by HIV. Denialists often use their critique of the link between HIV and AIDS to promote alternative medicine as a cure, and attempt to convince HIV-infected individuals to avoid anti-retroviral (ARV) therapy in favour of vitamins, massage, yoga and other unproven treatments.

In 2000, when the International AIDS Conference was held in Durban, Mbeki convened a Presidential Advisory Panel containing a number of known AIDS denialists. Panel meetings were closed to the general press. At these meetings doctors heard calls from advocates calling for HIV testing to be legally banned and were treated to presentations that were far removed from African medical reality. At the same conference, President Mbeki made a speech that attracted much criticism in that he avoided references to HIV and instead focused mainly on poverty as a powerful co-factor in AIDS diagnosis, leading hundreds of delegates to walk out on his speech. Mbeki also sent a letter to a number of world leaders likening the mainstream AIDS research community to supporters of the apartheid regime. The tone and content of Mbeki's letter led diplomats in the US to initially question whether it was a hoax. AIDS scientists and activists were dismayed at the President's attitude and responded with the Durban Declaration, a document affirming that HIV causes AIDS, signed by over 5,000 scientists and physicians from around the world.

His administration was repeatedly accused of failing to respond adequately to the AIDS epidemic, including failing to authorise and implement a national treatment programme including making cheap anti-retroviral medicines available to all public hospitals in SA, which can be directly linked to the death of thousands of people. In particular his ban extended to an anti-retroviral programme to prevent HIV transmission from pregnant mothers to babies while in the womb.

It was in November 2003, only after the Cabinet had overruled the President, that the Government finally approved a plan to make anti-retroviral treatment publicly available.

The former South African health minister Manto Tshabalala-Msimang also attracted heavy criticism, as she often promoted nutritional remedies such as garlic, lemons, beetroot and olive oil to people suffering from AIDS, while emphasising possible toxicities of anti-retroviral drugs, which she has referred to as 'poison'. The South African Medical Association accused Tshabalala-Msimang of 'confusing a vulnerable public'. In September 2006, a group of over 80 scientists and academics called for 'the immediate removal of Dr. Tshabalala-Msimang as Minister of Health and for an end to the disastrous, pseudoscientific policies that have characterised the South African Government's response to HIV/AIDS.' In December 2006, deputy health minister Nozizwe Madlala-Routledge described 'denial at the very highest levels' over AIDS. She was subsequently fired by Mbeki.

In 2008, Mbeki was ousted from power. The new President installed Barbara Hogan as Health Minister, who immediately voiced shame at the Mbeki Government's embrace of AIDS denialism and vowed a new course, stating: 'The era of denialism is over completely in South Africa.'

This story vividly portrays how our beliefs can cause us to gravitate to people who share or align with our views; refuse to open our views to scrutiny by others; remove people from teams who do not hold the same views; and attack those we cannot remove. We also attract people who have similar beliefs which then reinforces and deepens our own beliefs. We then lose our ability to adopt a concerned, compassionate and balanced perspective on the dire consequences that holding on to our beliefs may be causing.

The Challenge

In a company, dominant beliefs often become the moral compass. However even the most successful companies can become captured or hijacked down a dead-end track without knowing it. This is because the culture we are immersed in is ubiquitous to our thinking. Over time successful companies develop distinctive business ideologies, doctrines or beliefs that shape how they operate, often referred to by employees as how things are done around here. This then becomes a dominant logic that few challenge.

The same applies to successful leaders, whose dominant logic – a biased lens through which they perceive, see and interpret the world – can after a while become an inflexible tautology that no one challenges. They consequently become unable to adapt to change. This then can lead to derailment of even the most successful executives as shown by TalentInvest's research that went into the book *Derailed! How Successful Leaders Stay on Track,* by the author.[2]

Such biases, at the collective and individual levels (often operating at a largely unconscious subliminal level) are easily formed,,questioned only when there is a breach or breakdown in values. This questioning often comes too late to avert damage to the clients, market, industry and community at large. Company loyalty often becomes the proxy for support of dominant logic.

Many companies try to instill loyalty in their employees to 'the way we do things around here'. But it's safe to say few of them took it as far as IBM. As a somewhat noble belief, IBM founder Thomas Watson Sr was of the opinion that if a company is based on its own set of values, based on what it is rather than what it makes, it allows the company to change with the times. On the face of it this made a lot of sense. But in fact this belief came to rob IBM of several decades of its market leadership, before it found its way back again.

From as early as 1914, under CEO Thomas J. Watson, IBM employees had to learn company songs, go through lengthy training and participate in family outings. They prided themselves on being obsessively focused on their customers' needs. To blend in with their clients they wore plain white shirts and blue suits. IBM was something more than a company. It was a mission. 'You know, we do not consider or think of IBM as a business, as a corporation, but IBM as a great world institution that has work to do,' Watson said at the New York World's Fair in 1939. A dark (or grey) suit, white shirt, and a 'sincere' tie was the public uniform for IBM employees for most of the twentieth century. All its recruits came from a few choice top-flight universities.

Coupled with this strong unifying corporate culture, its computer technology turned IBM into a corporate powerhouse. Under Thomas Watson Jr, who succeeded his father's 40 years of leadership, the company was run with religious fervor. IBM poured a lot of the money it made into research and development, and for years its nine labs churned out a dazzling array of new products and still holds the largest number of patents of any other US company. Famous inventions by IBM include the automated teller machine (ATM), the floppy disk, the hard disk drive, the magnetic stripe card, the DRAM chip and computer languages like Fortran.

However, for all its success and employee engagement, the seeds of trouble had been planted. Its values and corporate culture became a millstone around its neck resulting in it not seeing or responding fast enough to the profound changes taking place in the market or challenging how it had always done things. It was also seduced by the huge amounts of money it was making from mainframes, and failed to anticipate the personal computer revolution. Kevin Maney, commissioned by IBM to co-author *Making the World Work Better*,[3] says challengers like Microsoft and Apple were nipping at its heels while 'The IBM-ers were still showing up in their suits and white shirts, thinking that was part of being an IBM-er. The hot guns from the Silicon Valley companies were showing up in their Birkenstocks and jeans and T-shirts'.

By the early 1990s, IBM was losing billions a year, and for the first time it had to lay off thousands of people. The IBM way had shaped how it competed, how it structured itself, how it measured performance and of course how it thought about itself and the business it was in. This became their dominant logic, understood by all in the company and described as 'how things are done around here'. But over time this dominant logic became orthodoxy that no one challenged, until in 1993 Louis V. Gerstner Jnr was brought in to transform the company, presiding over the most radical change programme in US corporate history.

Gerstner is credited with saving IBM from going out of business by refocusing IBM on its IT services business. He challenged the conventional business (impossible had he been an insider) reviving a culture that had become moribund, and transforming it into a broad-based IT integrator. Gerstner's book *Who Says Elephants Can't Dance?*[4] gives a sense of the agonising deliberations with the traditional IBM stalwarts about what to sell and what to keep and what to bulk up. It took an outsider like Gerstner without the 'baggage' or prior attachment to any strategy to challenge some of the underlying values that were holding IBM back; from the IBM uniform to the view that the mainframe business was dead and the personal computer business was its future. He redefined its mission by challenging IBM's dominant logic and countering biased judgement.

A Closer Look

Beliefs can fail us. But to understand how they fail us we have to know how they work. So let's start with the definition.

We refer to something as a belief – a conviction about something that matters to us – like religion, ethics, policies or a belief in the good of others. These are explicit beliefs in that we know we hold them. When in question we can often articulate them and defend them if we need to. That is to say there is a feeling we experience associated with a belief. But there are also beliefs we don't experience – they are our mental models of the world.

OUR MENTAL MODELS

At a simple level, we carry a mental model that our car will take us from A to B or that the lights will turn on when we flick a switch – mental representations of our physical, social and emotional world – models of the world we take for granted but that help us make predictions and assume consequences on the strength of those predictions.

However beliefs (mental models) can have consequences as we saw in the Greenspan case described in Chapter 2. In fact our beliefs are inextricable from our identities. Which is why when counsellors and psychologists work with a patient on their self-limiting beliefs they work at the level of beliefs about ourselves (self-concept) in order for the patient to let go of limiting beliefs that may be destroying their life. It is also why our sense of self is so badly wounded when our beliefs are proved to be wrong. So regardless of whether we hold them consciously or unconsciously they influence how we behave.

We become conscious of them when something does not turn out like we imagined. Imagine you are meeting someone at a cafe (after having had an email relationship with them for some time). During this email relationship you have built a mental picture of this person. You then turn up at the cafe and they are nothing like you imagined. What has happened is that you have conflated all of your mental images of this person into a single human being without being aware you have built this person. And then it turns out to be completely wrong. This is a form of sophisticated theory making in progress, without you ever being aware of it.

Our mental models are a powerful part of our belief systems and can blind us to other possibilities.

HOW WE PERCEIVE THE MENTAL MODELS OF OTHERS

We tend to think of the beliefs or mental models of other people as self-serving but never our own. We see our objectivity but not that of others, we see our rationality but not that of others and we see reality in our beliefs but not in the beliefs of others. Let's take this a step further.

We tend to conclude that those who don't see the world the way we do don't have the right information and the exposure to correct this. However when we reject their beliefs we think it is good judgement on our part. It is not uncommon for us to hear ourselves and others say of people who don't believe what we do that they 'don't live in the real world'. What we really mean is that they don't live in our model of the world – they don't share our vision of how things are. But by doing this we are denying that they have the same intellectual capability or moral judgement as we have. In fact we deny the significance or even the value of their life experience from which their beliefs arise. Our behaviour does not just stop at dismissal of others. We also use our mental models to influence our actions towards others.

As an illustration, an executive facing the task of managing the performance of a team member may in effect work from two quite different mental models. One based on respect for what people do (let's call this conditional respect) and another model on respect for who people are (unconditional respect). An executive who operates on the first mental model will value team members for what they deliver,'I respect you because you deliver for me' that is, a cog in the wheel or a driver of profit and the like. This will influence the kind of conversation they are capable of having with the team member. That is, they will as a consequence adopt a different approach to managing performance from the executive working off the second model. Someone working on the basis of the second model, that is, 'I respect you because of who you are' will hold a more compassionate view, working collaboratively and inclusively to improve performance with a 'we are all in this together' approach. We can see clearly in this illustration how our behaviour can be profoundly driven by our mental models and bias our approach and interactions with others in the workplace.

OUR VERSION OF THE TRUTH

We often rationalise away the differences in beliefs and mental models on three counts:

- the other person's ignorance;

- the other person's stupidity;

- the other person's immorality.

Alan Greenspan (discussed more fully in Chapter 2) did not consider that his views may be dangerous but considered that people who doubted the free market capitalist model were dangerous and had to be silenced. Our beliefs can act as powerful filters of reality and provide us our version of the truth, discounting the versions of others and thereby further entrenching our beliefs even in the face of counter-evidence.

Evidence that fits with one's beliefs is quickly accepted as sound and counter-evidence is doubted and submitted for close interrogation. Cordelia

Fine describes this phenomenon in her book *A Mind of Its Own*.[5] She builds on this and other similar research about beliefs saying, 'As a result people can wind up holding their beliefs even more strongly after seeing counterevidence. We think, "if that's the best that the other side can come up with then I really must be right". This phenomenon called belief polarisation, she asserts, may help explain why attempting to disillusion people of their perverse misconceptions is often futile'. The reality is that we find research convincing and sound if its results happen to align with or confirm our beliefs and we find research shoddy and flawed if the results fail to confirm our beliefs. This is true not only of beliefs about life in general but also has significant saliency for the way we think through and make decisions in business today.

SELF-FULFILLING AND SELF-PERPETUATING

But this values bias has one other insidious impact that we must mention here found more often in business today than we think. Possibly the most worrying of these is the self-fulfilling prophecy which often works very silently. In a now well-known experiment by Robert Rosenthal and Lenore Jacobson[6] a group of children were given a fake test which was claimed to be a measure of intellectual potential. Then, supposedly on the basis of the test results, they told teachers that the following children would be displaying an intellectual blossoming over the next few months. In fact these children were randomly selected from a class list. Yet the teachers' expectation of these children as being better than the rest, actually led to a real and measurable enhancement of their intellect over the ensuing months. The teachers engaged 'more deeply' with and taught 'more warmly' the students whom they had greater expectations of, leading to evidence of real blossoming and faster development of these students. The powerful impact that a particular teacher's prejudice and stereotype is not only self-fulfilling, it is self-perpetuating.

This kind of self-fulfilling and self-perpetuating phenomenon is not only true of teachers in the classroom but of leaders in companies today. Those who get on to a company's talent programme, even if picked using shoddy assessment methodologies, are given 'special mentoring' and 'shown the ropes' and provided access to experiences that allow them to develop and unlock their potential more quickly. As the notion of their talent becomes comfortably established in the minds of the company and its executives, it puts these 'special' people on a self-perpetuating cycle as they are given greater and greater access to the best development opportunities. TalentInvest's work with companies to tighten their talent identification processes is driven by this concern about how our beliefs relating to who is talented and who is not, if not calibrated well, can lead to a generation of young leaders who are more likely to derail. This can also result in others who stagnate, not because they are not talented but because they were denied the early development they deserved.

Therefore our beliefs can not only influence the quality of our own decisions, they can influence the outcomes for others, just as others' beliefs can influence and control our judgements and actions without our knowledge, as the Rosenthal experiment above shows.

Close Up

We present two real case scenarios, both of which demonstrate the impact of values on decision making. For obvious reasons these scenarios, while keeping close to the accuracy of the circumstances, have details changed in order to protect confidentiality.

CASE 1

Insufficient attention is paid at the integration stage to the cultural norms, beliefs and values inherent in the merging partners. This causes many mergers to fail. A 2004 Bain and Co. study showed that 70 per cent of all mergers failed to create value. A stand out and well-documented case is the high-profile merger in 1998 of the German-based automaker Daimler Benz AG and the third largest automaker in the US, American-based Chrysler Corporation, to create the fifth largest automaker. It was demerged, at huge costs to the shareholders, three years later.

These were two very strong and yet different organisational cultures, characterised also by two styles of automaking, two approaches to business and two proud but distinct national cultures and the accompanying differences in value systems. Guergen Schrempp, the CEO of Daimler-Benz, and Robert Eaton, the Chrysler Corp CEO, saw great synergies in combining Daimler-Benz's engineering skills, technological advancement and focus on quality with Chrysler's skills in innovation, speed of product development and bold marketing style. It was likened to a 'marriage made in heaven'.

In the end the culture clash, however, was not just a clash of products, brands and values. It resulted in a clash of employees. At one end was the

Germanic-disciplined style of engineering and uncompromising quality and after-service care; on the other end was Chrysler's assertive risk-taking cowboy aura. The dislike and distrust was clear, with some Daimler-Benz executives publically saying that they would never drive a Chrysler, just one of several cultural difficulties eroding away any chance of realising synergy value.

Schrempp asked for extensive analysis and assessment of potential merger candidates (both internally and externally) but had long before settled on Chrysler as his choice. In fact, when consultants told him that his strategy was unlikely to create shareholder value, he dismissed the data and went ahead with his plans. Schrempp may have solicited views from many parties, but he clearly failed to give those views much weight. His mind had been made up, and while going through the motions of providing others a voice and input, he had failed to subject those views to thoughtful consideration. Specifically he had failed to recognise the challenges that the integration of two very different value systems would pose.

Three years later, Daimler Chrysler's market capitalisation stood at US$44 billion, approximately the same value as Daimler-Benz before the merger. Its stock banished from the S&P 500 index and Chrysler Group's share value declined by one-third relative to pre-merger values.

Schrempp's decision bias

In a steady state, underlying beliefs and values generally don't present any issues. It is when they are put under pressure, in this case by the merger of two very different organisational cultures, that it becomes clear what a profound effect beliefs and values can have on decisions. Unless we reflect more deeply on the dominant logic, beliefs and values we bring to the table, our decisions can have unintended consequences, in some instances with catastrophic consequences.

What decision might have produced a different, game-changing outcome?

Could a cultural analysis pre-merger have averted the disaster? It is hard to say. The integration team and senior leaders could have been provided some deep cultural fluency training (not just cultural sensitivity which is focused on awareness, cultural fluency on the other hand is focused on turning that awareness into skills). This would have better prepared the respective teams on the required nuances in style and approach. Additionally, in leading the integration, the CEO could have tempered euphoria and optimism about the deal with the many risks that bringing together very different core values and capabilities, business models and operating paradigms, and cultures held. A more systematic review of risks could have suggested a different strategy altogether – and a recalibrating of the synergies that could have been extracted. A genuine awareness of the differences and complimentarity of the business values of both companies could have preceded genuine collaboration. Integrated platforms and joint projects could have channeled the best of both cultures and operating principles in the interests of strengthening the combined entity. Quite aside from the fundamental question of how the integration could have been better planned or approached, the bigger question and choice could have been to manage the entities separately for a time before trying to determine how best to leverage core capabilities, which would have provided the requisite 'soak time' to determine how best to integrate.

CASE 2

Jane had joined Arco Ltd from a well-known accounting firm where she had a good grounding in financial risk and compliance. She had been instantly recognised as talented and was moved after 18 months into the financial strategy area of the company to work on a major ongoing project to drive up the profitability of the company. She recognised the level of support that this project had not just with senior management but with the Board. She also recognised that there were some inherent contradictions in the sustainability of the growth strategies Arco was pursuing.

Jane's experience of the culture over the past year was that it was restless, relentless and short-term oriented. She discovered that few people in Arco had time for thinking about longer-term sustainability. It was about success here and now. 'Tomorrow will take care of itself' appeared to be the modus operandi. There was also a worrying tendency to pay attention to the shareholder's short-term needs (in an effort to drive up the share price) and ignore other stakeholders. Arco also had a talent acceleration programme that resulted in talent moving on relatively quickly, solely on the strength of their revenue outcomes and not on the values they demonstrated. Additionally those identified as top talent were progressed before they were ready or had properly consolidated their performance, as reward for performance (not as recognition of talent).

She had also heard on the grapevine market information that suggested that a couple of investors were starting to look more closely at Arco's reporting of its profits, including the highly leveraged bonus schemes (linked to stock price) that had been put in place over the last three years to drive up revenues. While she recognised that these investors were known to be 'activists', she felt it was her duty as an officer of the company to raise this information, even though she had obtained this information via informal channels.

She took the opportunity to raise her views with the Executive Committee at one of the strategy briefings she had participated in. Because of the credibility she had built (she was after all on Arco's fast track programme) there was an eagerness to engage with her concerns, as she discovered following that meeting. The COO and the head of one of the largest divisions paid her a visit to have a 'chat' about how the briefing had gone. They pointed out to her that the external auditors (not however the one she had worked with before) were zealous and poured over the accounts and that the concerns she had heard were unfounded, mischievous and motivated by one of the investors wanting a seat on the Board. They also pointed out to Jane that, despite Arco's success, it was not as profitable as its rivals and this was something that ought to be more of a concern than what activist shareholders were thinking about.

It was about two years after this conversation and two years after she had taken on this role when alarm bells started to ring for her. There was in her view some overstating of the profit numbers that she was not comfortable with. She sent a note to her boss who said she was worrying about nothing, adding that if she continued to have concerns he was happy to speak to the auditors himself. She indicated that she would like to be at that meeting. However such a meeting did not materialise despite her following it up with her boss. Jane then decided to send an email to the CEO stating her concerns in writing and saying that leading up to the interim half year results she felt it was a good time to 'take a hit' with the profit numbers.

The CEO called her in and at first it felt like an amicable chat. However she got a distinct feeling he was trying to 'rough her up' when he said to her that both their bonuses were dependent on profit numbers being ahead of the industry average. He continued that while she was on the talent programme and had enjoyed extensive investment from the company (a three-month Harvard programme she had been sent on the previous year), that her ability to 'stick with the programme' was an essential aspect to this continuing investment in her personal development. Jane left the room feeling decidedly uncomfortable.

Jane thought long and hard about her situation and her need as a single mother to get her daughter through expensive private school and the associated fee burden. She rationalised to herself that the activists were smart enough to find what they were looking for and that the situation would 'take care of itself', without her help or intervention.

At the annual results six months later, and unbeknown to the executives of the company or to Jane (her sources seemed to have dried up), a number of investors demanded and got a change in the Board and audit/risk committee positions. Analysts and commentators appeared to become aware that there were 'some issues' with the reporting of the underlying profit. The share price received a hammering. There was a subsequent change in management. Jane left the company feeling somewhat relieved that it was over.

Jane's decision bias

Jane was swept up by the 'systems of meaning' (described in detail in the next chapter) that was being spun around Arco Ltd. The dominant logic was 'profit above all', that is, that maximising profit was the right thing to do in all circumstances. Any questioning of this logic, such as questions about an alternative logic based on finding a sustainable level of growth, was dismissed or rationalised away or regarded as disloyal. Pressure on Jane to 'fall in line' ranged from subtle to not so subtle. In the end this story had a happy ending, although the change did not come from inside the company. The pressure from two investors agitating for necessary change, achieved it, bringing about an end to a dominant logic that could have very easily destroyed the company. At a personal level, Sarah was faced with a values dilemma requiring her to make a choice between the value of job security and her value of professional integrity, which she resolved against her better judgment.

What decision might have produced a different, game-changing outcome?

Both the Board and executive management of the company needed to balance short-term and long-term success and determine for both what would be a reliable measure of success (they are necessarily different). Regular leadership forums that allowed the executives to dialogue freely about the robustness of the corporate/business strategy, scenario-planning different futures or challenging 'world views' would have allowed the leadership to recognise that there was not just one way of building a successful company. The Board, in turn, responsible for ensuring growth was sustainable, could have taken a closer look at where growth was coming from and challenged the CEO more often on the sustainability of growth streams. Additionally, rather than creating an environment where dissent was seen as disloyal, the CEO could also have cultivated a culture where dissent was itself used as critical monitor of risk. Linking bonus to stock price introduced a particular bias which had the potential to create short-term thinking, bad behavior and unhealthy trade offs.

Red Flags

You will know when underlying beliefs and values may be playing its part in biasing decision making when you see the following:

- the 'we have always done it this way' narrative;

- the failure to challenge one's own and others' mental models;

- assuming that you have the monopoly of the truth (in a given situation);

- the failure to question the existing values; unquestioning acceptance of current company values;

- the failure to recognise or underestimate the cultural complexities associated with a merger of two entities;

- the lack of consistency in the values/beliefs underpinning the decisions made;

- strong opposition to the underlying beliefs of others;

- blind faith in a theory/approach and the unpreparedness to question it;

- subtle pressure exerted on people to fall into line with the dominant logic of the company;

- bonus programmes that drive short-term behavior and unsustainable growth.

Success Strategies

Success strategies we suggest in order to neutralise the impact entrenched beliefs can have in leading you astray when making decisions include the following:

Rethink the mindset

- Challenge your mental model.

- Recognise that you may not hold the monopoly of the truth in any given situation – that we all hold pieces of the truth.

- Challenge your self-fulfilling or self-perpetuating judgments.

- Encourage internal challenge/discussion of dominant market logic (dominant logic is often invisible and needs to be surfaced and debated).

- Carry out a check of your core beliefs and validate how successfully they have served you. A list created by Geoffrey James (a regular contributor to ChiefExecutive.net) following research he did with successful CEOs may help in this process:
  - management is service, not control;
  - my employees are my peers not my children;
  - motivation comes from vision not from fear;
  - business is an ecosystem, not a battlefield;
  - a company is a community, not a machine;
  - change equals growth not pain;
  - technology offers empowerment, not automation;
  - work should be fun not mere toil.

Rethink the players

- Ensure the independence of external advisors (independence in this case refers to the advisor not having a vested interest or benefitting in any way from the decision being made).

- Bring in independent experts to challenge the dominant logic.

Rethink the process

- Structure annual strategic reviews as occasions for strategic choices (already made) to be robustly debated.

- Reflect on the assumptions and assertions being made about 'how we do business' so that dominant belief systems can be surfaced, discussed and taken into consideration when decisions are made.

- Ask powerful questions of yourself and the team in order to deepen the conversation about values (especially when there is pressure on values):
  - What values are guiding our thinking?
  - What is the one value we/you are unwilling to give up?
  - What is the value that both you and the conflicting group believe you share?
  - What assumptions do we hold about each other and how will we test those assumptions?

- Regularly convene facilitated values conversations using hypothetical but realistic dilemmas in which values come under stress in order to openly discuss competing values and develop a shared view on these values and navigate such dilemmas that may arise from time to time.

Notes

1 Report published by Department of Immunology and Infectious Diseases; Harvard School of Public Health AIDS Initiative, 2008: Estimating the Lost Benefits of Antiretroviral Drug Use in South Africa by P. Chigwedere, MD, G. R. Seage III, ScD, MPH, S. Gruskin, JD, MIA, T-H. Lee, ScD, and M. Essex, DVM, PhD.
2 *Derailed! What Smart Executives Do to Stay on Top*, M. Thuraisingham, Blue Toffee, 2010.
3 *Making the World Better: The Ideas that Shaped a Century and Company*, K. Maney, S. Hamm and J. O'Brien, IBM Press–Pearson plc, 2005.
4 *Who Says Elephants Can't Dance?* L. V. Gerstner, Harper Collins Publishers, 2002.
5 *A Mind of Its Own*, C. Fine, Norton & Company, 2006.

6 *Robert Rosenthal and Lenore Jacobson – Pygmalion in the Classroom.* Holt,
   Rinehart and Winston, 1968; *Pygmalion in the Classroom* (Expanded ed.), New
   York: Irvington, 1992.

10

Power Can Corrupt

Challenging the myth that the more control or influence we have the better our decisions

Despite the attempts by regulators to stamp out cartels, unfortunately they are more prevalent than we would like to admit. A cartel is essentially an oligopoly that acts like a monopoly, powerful enough to set a price to maximise profit often at the expense of the end customer. These price-fixing behaviours are in effect an attempt to unfairly consolidate one's market power in order to keep others out of that market. By keeping others out of the market, they effectively keep prices high and increase their profits. It often acts against free market principles that allow enterprising new entrants to thrive and succeed. This abuse of power does not just exist at an industry level but also at a company, team and individual level where an individual can act in ways that consolidate their power base in an organisation creating uneven playing fields and unfair individual advantage. It is this search for more power that operates like a lens or filter through which they view the world and their place in it. Resulting decisions become biased, driven by no other reason than one's need to consolidate and increase power, often sabotaging the quality of decision, the consequence of which may only show up sometime in the future as in the cartel examples described .

De Beers was well known for its monopolistic practices throughout the twentieth century, using its dominant position to manipulate the international diamond market. The company used several methods to exercise this control over the market. Firstly, it convinced independent producers to join its single channel monopoly; secondly it flooded the market with diamonds similar to those of producers who refused to join the cartel; and lastly, it purchased and stockpiled diamonds produced by other manufacturers in order to control prices through supply. In 2000, the De Beers model changed, as a result of factors such as the decision by producers in Russia, Canada and Australia, to distribute diamonds outside of the De Beers channel, thus effectively ending the monopoly and the power of DeBeers – an unfolding reality that their power bias had blinded them to.

The Phoebus cartel was a cartel made up of, among others, Osram, Philips and General Electric from as far back as 1924 until 1939, controlling the manufacture and sale of light bulbs. The cartel reduced competition in the light bulb industry for almost 20 years, and has been accused of preventing technological advances that would have produced longer-lasting light bulbs earlier. This case is another interesting reflection of how cartels can blind members to opportunities they may be sitting on.

In the Phoebus case, decisions were taken to exploit market power, preventing innovation that could have transformed the industry and made its players much more successful. By looking through this power bias and making decisions that related to protecting and exploiting current products and markets they missed the chance to explore new products and new markets.

The most recent example of a cartel was between Unilever and Procter & Gamble who were found guilty of price fixing washing powder in eight European countries. The case was brought to the notice of the European Commission after a tip off from the Germany company, Henkel. The resulting penalties were heavy.

In submitting their defences most companies charged with cartel behaviour have claimed ignorance in some cases and in others claimed that some other external contextual issue caused something that resembled a cartel to develop. Whatever the reason, cartels only serve members and exploit the limited power that members outside the cartel enjoy, in the end however prospects for cartel members are damaged also, leaving aside reputational damage and financial costs. More importantly, any group or individual driven by power will see the world through this bias and lose necessary perspective as the examples above illustrate.

The Challenge

There is nothing wrong with power, until it creates an imbalance in decision making, blinding the decision maker to the consequences of those decisions on them as well as on the party (or parties) impacted by the decision. Such imbalances are common, and are often unintentionally created because decisions are not thought through enough. Your position of influence and power can blind you to the real consequences of the decision you are making. While most decision makers will seek to increase their influence in a given situation, they may not necessarily view their 'win–lose' decisions as unjust or unfair to other parties impacted by the decision. They will also sometimes rationalise away any disadvantage or hurt their decisions create for others. It is this blindness that we will explore in this chapter.

Power is relational in nature in that power in organisations is often defined by identity and structure or hierarchy. The conventional wisdom is that as one gets further up the hierarchy one accumulates more power and influence and can use it for decision making for both constructive or destructive purposes. This 'one up one down' thinking that plays out in most organisational decisions today can often obscure the real merits of an idea. For example, you may have an idea as an individual in the team but the idea still has to be assessed by your work group before it is accepted. This is power at play at the most basic level. Your idea may not see the light of day if others in your work groups or your line manager think the idea stinks. As this example shows, the use of power is not always readily observed in organisations. The reality is that power plays are usually subtle and hidden. Power in organisations can come from charisma (personality-related factors), from access to other sources of power (referred power) or from expertise.

Power can also reside in a division or functional team in ways that can lead to biased decision making. A company with a well-publicised and lauded reputation for a strong sales culture can sway decisions in ways that end up hurting the company. A dominant sales culture can result in sales people having disproportionate control over decisions about new products to take to market in comparison to the influence that the product development and R&D teams may have. This can cause products to be rushed to market without having been properly tested for the nuances of customer needs and tastes, which are valuable inputs that the R&D and product developers can bring to shape new product offerings. Sometimes it is not until an external party can get such a group to reflect on the dynamic around the decision-making table that the group recognises how the power of one group can directly or indirectly produce suboptimal decisions.

Patricia Bradshaw-Camball,[1] a well-known academic who researches power and politics, suggests that a key tactic that powerful groups/people use in organisations is to create 'systems of meaning' that others will accept. For example, in a meeting with other managers I might present only the information that supports my view of a situation. If the others accept my interpretation – my 'system of meaning' – I will have greater influence over the resulting decision-making process. Bradshaw-Camball for instance studied a hospital in which top management had created the illusion of a financial crisis to gain additional resources from the hospital's funding agency. By overstating the hospital's budget deficit by US$1.4 million and preventing department heads from seeing detailed, accurate financial reports, management created this false 'system of meaning' to gain an edge over competitor hospitals funded by the same agency. The illusion of a crisis was so effective that, in a study of workforce morale by an outside consultant, lower-level managers and employees said they were very concerned about the potential for cutbacks – the apparent reality. The consultant, not being informed of management's game plan, based his recommendations for the hospital upon this finding. His examination of the situation was insufficient to uncover the power and politics that were being played. A deeper examination of the history of the organisations and its relationships with various stakeholders, including those beyond its boundaries, can often uncover misleading 'facts' and the real 'systems of meaning' to which managers and employees subscribe.

A Closer Look

There are in essence two kinds of power both of which can result in biased or flawed decision making:

- structural or position power – derived from the authority vested in a given position or by virtue of a structure;

- personal or charismatic power – derived from the personal attributes of an individual.

Both can be used constructively or destructively. For example, structural power like cartels can wreak havoc for smaller less powerful industry players through the way in which that concentrated power is applied. Benefit for these players is often short lived. However structural power can also act as a positive force. An example is expert power, as is illustrated by the sway that the scientific community commands in society today. Their measure of influence is derived from their expertise, the same with the medical profession and so on. In a company, revenue generating units can hold powerful sway over non-revenue generating units or large units over smaller ones and so on.

Like structural power, personal power can also be used constructively or destructively. There are many leaders who have used their personal power, from Hitler at one extreme to Ghandi and Mandela at the other. Similar examples come to mind in the business arena, from Al Dunlap at one extreme to Jack Welch at the other extreme. Personal power, if accumulated in extreme, can be destructive both for the powerful and the overpowered.

However this dichotomy between structural and personal power can belie the complexity that can exist. Someone without any structural or position power can still acquire personal power that far exceeds the influence, in a decision-making sense, that is implicit in the role they occupy. For example, someone lower down in an organisation can have disproportionate and sometimes dangerous decision influence on people in powerful positions. There are some notable cases where boards of companies are later found to have been manipulated by a charismatic and strong-willed CEO, making decisions that took the company down a track it should never have gone down. However personal power can also be a positive force for change even at the societal level where the 'power of the people' has toppled many governments, even those not voted in by democratic traditions, as the 2010 'Arab Spring' demonstrated.

With both kinds of power, the biasing impact on decision making can be profound. The following are two examples of how power can actually influence negotiation and decision making. One is that it drives overconfidence and the other is that it can block change.

POWER DRIVES OVERCONFIDENCE

First let's look at the overconfidence issue. It is not power itself that tends to corrupt decision making. It is the overall sense of control and invincibility that comes with that power that tends to make people feel overconfident in their ability to make good decisions.

The more power a business leader thinks they have, the worse they get at calling the shots, new research shows. A study by University of Southern California Professor Nathanael Fast[2] has determined that, in the business world, unconstrained power can hinder decision making. 'The overall sense of control that comes with power tends to make people feel overconfident in their ability to make good decisions,' Fast said, noting the research aimed to make leaders more conscious of the pitfalls that they can fall prey to.

To explore this tendency, researchers conducted multiple experiments that manipulated power by randomly assigning participants to high-power or low-power roles. They were then asked to bet money on their ability to answer six trivia questions.

In the study, those who were made to feel powerful actually lost money betting on their knowledge, and those who didn't feel powerful took fewer betting risks and didn't lose their cash.

POWER CAN BLOCK CHANGE

Any consideration of organisational power needs to take into account the related topic of organisational politics. Politics is power in action and involves acquiring, developing and using power to achieve one's objectives. Political power is especially evident when organisations are undergoing change and when change threatens the existing balance of power in an organisation. Political power is used to maintain balance and block change. Powerful stakeholders can play a role in controlling who is talking to who, who has access to who, who has information on what, where ideas get bottlenecked, how ideas get spread, who has the ear of those in charge and so on.

The understanding of power in an organisation is often not served by looking at the organisation chart. It is the invisible networks of relationships that sit behind the organisation chart that often reveals where real power lies and how decisions can become seriously biased.

A systematic mapping of powerful individual stakeholders can show up the challenges, for example, decision bottlenecks associated with driving new ideas and change in any organisation. Powerful informal coalitions can be identified in a similar way. It is also important to look at interest groups that control key resources or 'have the numbers' to either directly or indirectly sway decisions. Powerful coalitions are seldom temporary; a reality that often dawns on leaders that have tried to work with change-resistant organisations. Decisions when made at the top become diffused as they are translated further down the organisation thereby diluting and eventually stalling the change momentum. This is why top management teams, and not just a couple of top managers, are often removed in a large change effort. Merely eliminating a couple of managers may not necessarily prevent the remainder of the team, often a long-standing, powerful coalition, from blocking the change.

Karen Stephenson, an anthropologist and social network theorist, now lecturing at Rotterdam School of Management, Erasmus University, studies how knowledge flows through those organisations alluding to trust as holding the tentacles of such invisible networks together. In her book *The Quantum Theory of Trust*[3] she shows how powerful networks in organisations are today and challenges the notion that they are random. Instead she maintains they are powerfully nuanced and reflect the secret life and power within knowledge-based organisations, ultimately impacting decisions, especially around change.

Decades of research on individual and group behaviour show that we socialise with those who are similar to us, support us and share our goals – trusted tribes. This has the impact of making us bolder than we should be about our ideas and ultimately our decisions, because we don't get push back from our circle of supporters. This tribal behaviour occurs more often in organisations than we like to admit and blocks change perceived to dilute the power of a given group.

TRUST CAN ACT AS AN IMPORTANT MODERATOR, SOMETIMES

Even where power is not balanced, trust can play an important part in the decision-making process. For example, if 'A has power over B to the extent that he can get B to do something B would not otherwise do', it can result in abuse of power unless there is trust between A and B. Trust can be defined as 'an expression of confidence in another person – a belief that you will not be put at risk, harmed or injured by his/her actions'. Trust is in fact the counterbalance to power and can become the 'bedrock' of good decision making. Trust however enjoys a complex relationship with the parties and can sometimes lead decision makers astray.

Trust can sometimes be misplaced in that once we decide that someone is trustworthy, other qualities about that person are subtly influenced and conceived as consistent with this favourable impression. We are prone to the so-called 'halo effect' which occurs when one positive characteristic of a person dominates the way that person is viewed by others. Decisions taken in this situation can become seriously biased and flawed because of a level of unquestioned faith and trust vocalised as 'she is one of us' or 'he thinks like us'. The concept of trust intertwines at some point with that of power: a person or group of persons then holds power vis-à-vis those who place trust in them. This often plays out as tribal behaviour.

Tribes (which may come in the form of past membership of a school, for example, Etonians or members of a political party, revenue generators in a company who differentiate themselves from those who manage cost centres, members of the College of Surgeons, trade unions or other groups) are defined by their tendency to overemphasise the similarities within the group and overemphasise the differences between groups (their group and other groups). Trust follows and they look out for each other placing that tribe in a more advantageous situation than those who are not members of that tribe. This phenomenon is often referred to as 'in-groups' and 'out-groups'. Decisions taken by the 'in-group' will frequently disadvantage those in the 'out-group'. The in-group typically controls through language used, norms, rules, political power, access, policies, rituals and so on. The in-group will perpetuate the notion of what is an 'ideal' member (of the group, company, society), and it usually looks like them. Often the existence of an in-group may be subliminal, that is, the in-group may not recognise or acknowledge their impact on out-groups or the disadvantage they may perpetuate for members of the out-group. In many cases the out-group will not have the power to defend itself from the in-group's discriminatory actions or behaviour. At the heart of this behaviour is the use of power.

Regulation, industry watch dogs and other bodies are set up to even out this power playing field. In organisations today the tribal nature of decisions can adversely impact the integrity of decisions. These influences may be covert in many cases, for example where an in-group's framing of the decision could submerge the real issues that ought to be debated, thereby continuing to consolidate the in-group's power and influence. This is the power bias at work.

Close Up

We present two real case scenarios, both of which demonstrate the impact of power on decision making. For obvious reasons these scenarios, while keeping close to the accuracy of the circumstances, have details changed in order to protect confidentiality.

CASE 1

The Pet Care Division of Fortis is the largest pet care business in the world and enjoys an impressive market share lead on its rivals.

Fortis itself is known globally as having a strong sales culture and this was evident also in the Pet Care Division. The Pet Care Division had maintained its market share lead in the face of generic lower-priced pet care brands and new niche players working with large veterinarian clinic chains. Its category dominance in 'mainstay' pet care products was unequalled.

It enjoyed deep relationships with distributors, largely because of the company's huge investment in sales capability and talent management and the investment in training it had made for decades. Its reputation for great sales practices was also the envy of many consumer product companies, who regularly visited its sales organisation in various parts of the world.

In order to strengthen its market dominance in pet care, Fortis had determined strategically that it would extend and innovate its traditional categories. Sales incentives were put in place to ramp up revenues from new product categories. This strategic choice was left to the regions to execute. In the Asia Pacific region it resulted in a flurry of activity and new products were quickly launched into the distributor channels. A high degree of confidence in the strategy was voiced by the Division's senior sales management.

However all was not well with the roll out of the strategy in the region. The new products failed to grab the attention of pet owners and the costs of pulling these new products out of the market were mounting. Additionally these product withdrawals were starting to impact their brand impact/presence in its dominant staple categories.

In working with the business teams that made new product decisions, the Organisational Behaviour Consultant that was engaged went back to the decision-making table to investigate how decisions about these new products were being made. They found an interesting dynamic playing out. As an outcome of the strong sales culture, something the organisation was known for and prided itself in, the sales and marketing leaders around the table played a dominant role in pushing their ideas forward about what would work and what would not work from a marketplace perspective. The power that emanated from this position of significant organisational influence (borne out of long-standing reputation for sales performance) meant that their voices were loud and impactful. So loud in fact that they drowned out the voices of the R&D and Product Development leaders around the table who were cautioning against running to the market prematurely without proper research and testing with pets and pet owners.

The process for successfully taking a new product to market reflected a different team dynamic in that the marketing and sales group would bring ideas to the table and once an idea was deemed to have merit, often based on very detailed market research and analysis, the R&D and Product Development functions were tasked with developing the product to launch stage. This involved identifying focus groups of pet owners and pets to test the new product formulas, making the necessary product changes, testing again, refining again and testing again. This took time and patience, not an attribute that the sales leaders were known for.

The decision-making dynamic at the Petcare Division however, was such that plans for further testing of the products were overruled by the action-oriented and persuasive vote from the sales and marketing leaders around the table, who appeared to be underestimating new and emerging consumer tastes and patterns, which in turn caused products to be launched before they were tested comprehensively in the marketplace. By failing to fully leverage the expertise and experience that each of these stakeholder groups brought to the table, the resulting decisions were suboptimal. This was an example of the power and influence of one function swaying the decision-making process in a way that resulted in costly product failures.

The Sales Division's decision bias

The Sales Division, having enjoyed decades of successful sales performance at Fortis and having been showcased for its best-in-class practices, saw little need to question the limitations inherent in their 'world view' and contributions to important decisions that the company made. In not recognising the equal role and equal value that other divisions played in Fortis's success, it was subconsciously overriding any valuable perspectives or constructive views that other groups brought to the table with a 'we know the market best' attitude. This 'philosophical' divide had not been as pronounced because, up until this point, the strategic focus had been on strengthening existing categories and products, rather than launching new ones. In fact discussions about the new products resembled polarised debates (generating compromises) rather than dialogues (generating genuine collaboration).

What decision might have produced a different, game-changing outcome?

The consultants engaged by Fortis created a team intervention during which the decision-making group was able to reflect (as a group) on their respective thinking preferences and how these preferences might play out when faced with complex problems requiring breakthrough thinking. Preferences (as defined by the diagnostic tool Foursight© used in this process) do not guarantee ability nor does lack of preference suggest lack of ability but instead measures one's preference for essential components of the breakthrough thinking process. The theory underpinning this tool was that challenges will be creatively solved by engaging in the entire four-stage breakthrough thinking process, starting with Ideation, followed by Clarification, Development and finally Implementation. A high preference simply suggested that this is a part of the breakthrough thinking process that the individual felt most comfortable with and most energised by.

By getting each individual in the group to reflect on their own thinking preferences, the consultants were able to demonstrate how those preferences might be influencing their perspectives, positions and ultimately impacting the business decisions they made. The sales leaders were strong Ideators (came up with brilliant ideas) and Implementers (jumped into action), while the more deliberate and analytical attributes of the R&D leaders (mostly Clarifiers) were better at pinpointing the right problems to solve and the product developers (mostly Developers) were focused on building and fine tuning workable solutions. As a consequence of greater awareness and deeper insight into their own and others' preferences, the sales leaders took steps to allow their peers (in R&D and Product Development) an equal voice, collaborating in a way that leveraged the strengths that the entire team brought to the table. This allowed a more inclusive and constructive dialogue to emerge.

Through this kind of external team-based facilitation and feedback on the thinking preferences of individuals, teams are often able to gain invaluable insight into the kind of problem solver they are and the sort of teams they best thrive in. It will also help anticipate road blocks in the creative process, recognise the reasons for frustration in team processes, even out any unhelpful power plays and make more explicit the path to better, more creative solutions.

CASE 2

With the emergence of Asia and the Tiger economies, Bruce Tang founded Apex Telecommunications, producing and selling mobile telephony services in Singapore. In 1992 he was among the top three sector players in the city state. Based on the rapid growth of his business and strong cash flow position,

Bruce felt the time was right to take the company to the next level and build his regional ambition. In 1994 he launched his Asia expansion plan, acquiring businesses in Malaysia, Thailand, Hong Kong and Taiwan. By 1997 Apex was well established as a leader and company to watch in the region.

The management navigated through the Asian Crisis skillfully and, because it was cash rich, it could leverage the fact that competitors were struggling to increase market share. In 2002, the strong performance of Apex attracted the interest of ScanPoint, the Scandinavian-based European leader in the telecommunications market, which was looking to expand in Asia. With an acquisition in mind, ScanPoint launched a strategic due diligence study to understand Apex's core competences and its drivers of success to determine if in fact it had a sustainable model post Asian Crisis. The due diligence process showed a positive picture in the capability, resourcefulness and connections of Apex's management team.

In October 2002 Sven Johanssen, the CEO of ScanPoint met Bruce Tang (now the major shareholder of Apex) and key members of his management team in Dubai to explore a potential acquisition offer. There was an immediate rapport between the two CEOs. Sven was impressed with what he saw as a dynamic forward-looking management team. During the subsequent discussions and acquisition process, the quality of Bruce and the management was consistently evidenced which helped Sven build a strong investment case to his Board, and the decisions on both sides were quickly made and sealed. As part of the deal, Bruce and his team had to stay for at least five years to ensure stability and market confidence.

Meanwhile Sven, the ScanPoint CFO, questioned the high retention and bonus packages being paid to all but two of Bruce's executive team but was convinced by Bruce that these had been built into the acquisition business plan and were linked to performance. Convinced by the synergy potential and in order to establish a base of understanding and trust, Bruce invited Sven regularly to Singapore. Over the following months, Sven spent almost 50 per cent of his time there. The European management team was kept informed on progress in Asia on a regular basis.

By July 2003, ScanPoint was one of the leaders in the Asian telecommunications market, winning many public sector tenders. This was strategically important to the Group given the slowdown that many western economies were experiencing.

The acquisition plan detailed how the new Asian entity would be completely integrated and aligned with ScanPoint's operational platforms and management standards. Therefore, it came as a surprise during the 2004 budget discussion in October 2003 that Bruce proposed keeping the Asian entity separate. Furthermore despite the acquisition of Apex being funded largely through debt, Bruce mounted the argument that the debt should not appear on his balance sheet as it would be demotivating for his Asian team because of its impact on bonus allocations. Sven agreed but it caused consternation with the other two major divisional heads based in Europe who felt that Bruce was being given too many concessions. For example, Sven agreed that Asia need not implement the Client Management System (CMS) being rolled out across the group. There was no logic to this as the CMS allowed the group to track and account for any potential cross-subsidisation between the divisions. Rather than dealing directly with his divisional peers or with the CFO on cross-divisional issues, Bruce appeared to prefer to deal directly with Sven. Bruce also provided Sven with orchestrated exposure to his executives, positioning them in Sven's mind as potential successors to the Group Executive. Other members of Sven's executive team were starting to feel that Bruce's own team had more exposure and direct access to Sven than they had. Management team discussions became less constructive, decisions appeared more biased in favour of Asia even when there was no business rationale to support it. It seemed progressively to Bruce's peers like turf protection by Bruce and not about the Group's success. A more sinister explanation started to emerge in the corridors in Copenhagen suggesting that Bruce was using the Group's balance sheet to fund Apex's expansion into Asia, while retaining his cash within his region.

Sven, recognising the rift in his management team, encouraged the European management team to invest time to visit Singapore with an open mind. Meanwhile Sven (who had not spent any significant time in Asia prior to this acquisition) was visiting Singapore each month, spending a week to ten days at a time there, during which time Bruce went out of his way to wine and dine him and show him around Asia.

Bruce's decision bias

Bruce had leveraged the acquisition process to spend a large amount of time with Sven who was increasingly impressed by what he saw in Singapore and throughout Asia. Bruce clearly had a disproportionate influence over Sven who progressively made decisions which were perceived by others as lacking sound rationale and logic and seemed one sided, that is, biased towards Asia.

Eventually the rifts became so wide that one of the major division heads asked for early retirement (later joining a competitor) and the other major division head became disengaged and showed little compulsion to attend any of the meetings. Bruce progressively consolidated his power base by winning the confidence of Sven who by then had formed a close attachment to Asia. Bruce's decision bias was one of power and every move he made was driven by his need to consolidate his own power in the Asia region and fund his expansion in Asia off the Group's balance sheet, rather than showing any interest in Apex Technologies' broader global influence and success.

What decision might have produced a different, game-changing outcome?

Sven could have taken a less euphoric, more balanced approach to running what was to be a globally integrated business, rather than be swayed by the Asia story and his progressively close attachments to the region. To do this he may have needed to push back on Bruce's predisposition to be left alone to run his business and been more astute in seeing Bruce's game-plan for what it was. The Board and the CEO could have worked more cohesively, to ensure strategic coherence, working to an agreed and more balanced approach to the company's progress globally, vigilant about the risk of the Asia story overshadowing the importance to Apex of its other regions and geographies. Sven and the Board could also have been clearer in their articulation of the plan to extract value from this acquisition and stuck to that plan, rather than be swayed by Bruce's power-driven manoeuvres.

Red Flags

You will know when power may be playing its part in biasing decision making when you see the following:

- ambiguity intolerant people or authoritarians in personality/style;

- someone reacting negatively when they are challenged;

- unwillingness to open up one's own thinking to the scrutiny of others;

- strong self-interest implicit in the decisions made;

- 'gatekeeper' behaviour and the tendency to block access to people or information;

- decisions that are rarely challenged; reluctance to challenge strategy/approach;

- political factions and political game playing;

- the existence of 'in-groups' and 'out-groups';

- decisions that are frequently relitigated after they have been decided at a meeting of the decision makers;

- the tendency (when dealing with peers of subordinates) to use referred authority (from superiors), rather than one's own personal influence;

- a low level of trust in the culture and a belief that there are never any candid conversations.

Success Strategies

Success strategies we suggest in order to neutralise the impact of personal or position/structural power on decision making include the following:

Rethink the mindset

- Reflect on the extent to which, in the pursuit of goals, you have recognised and invested in building trust with others.

- Being continuously alert to your personal interests and ensuring that they are not getting in the way of sound judgment or good decision.

- Recognise your tendency to react negatively when your views are challenged.

- Challenge your need to micromanage and manipulate outcomes in order to unfairly consolidate your power or your influence.

Rethink the players

> • Surround yourself with people who are willing to speak truth to power.
>
> • Build a competent and capable management team, able to challenge the hierarchy in constructive ways.

Rethink the process

> • Institute strong governance mechanisms including audit/ enforcement disciplines.
>
> • Create clear delegated authorities, that ensure decision-making processes are transparent and can be consistently applied.
>
> • Distribute power evenly across your direct reports so that no one direct report has significantly more power and responsibility than their peers which can adversely impact team cohesion and collaboration.
>
> • Conduct a deeper examination of the history of the organisation and its relationships to stakeholders in order to uncover misleading 'facts' and the real 'systems of meaning' to which people subscribe.

Notes

1 Culture, Leadership and Power: The Keys to Organisational Change, R. W. Clement, *Business Horizons*, 1994.
2 Power and Overconfident Decision-Making, N. Fast, N. Sivanathan and N Mayer, *Journal Organizational Behavior and Human Decision Processes*, Nov 2011.
3 The Quantum Theory of Trust, Karen Stephenson, reprinted in *Strategy+Business Magazine* 2002.

PART III

Developing Best Practice Decision Behaviour

11

Best Practice Decision Behaviour

'Diversity in Counsel, Unity in Command.'

Cyrus the Great, Founder of the Persian Empire,
Military Leader, 6th Century BC

In the previous eight chapters we looked closely at many of the risks and pitfalls we face as decision makers and the high costs of biased judgments and bad decisions. In this chapter we will focus on the process itself, in particular the time decision makers invest in the process of arriving at a better decision.

Decision making as a process is faced with two big challenges:

- the failure of the process to generate enough (decision) options;

- options generated are not evaluated robustly enough.

While these two challenges are influenced by the time decision makers allocate to the process of making a decision, it is also influenced by the decision behaviour or skills they demonstrate, even when time is on their side. Both these challenges have implications for how the process is designed and also the kind of thinking that is employed in the process. This chapter will open with examining these implications more closely before pulling together and consolidating the concrete behavioural actions we have advocated in previous chapters.

The best practice we advocate in this chapter is predicated on the important assumption that the process, that is, the conversation or dialogue around the decision-making table, is as important as the outcome. That is to say that we should care about the process of decision making as much as we care about the end outcome we are aiming for.

The Criticality of the Process for Team-based Decisions

Research by McKinsey in 2010 shows that the biggest impact on the quality of most decisions we make in organisations today is the quality of the conversation or dialogue leading up to the decision rather than the data itself. Their research was based on the study of over 1,000 business decisions and reported in full in March 2010 *McKinsey Quarterly*. It reflects what we know to be true of our experience of organisations.

Good decisions result from the conscious exercising of choice. In particular when decisions are made in teams, there are three ingredients necessary for good decisions to emerge:

- fresh insight

- independent thought

- robust debate.

However, for these three ingredients to exist in the decision-making process, an environment or decision culture needs to be created that is open and participative: a culture where fresh insight is welcomed even when it cuts across prevailing thinking or dominant logic, where the lone, contrary or dissenting voice can speak freely, and everyone, without fear or favour can confidently and robustly debate the alternative views on problem definition, search for and explore multiple solutions, and finally choose the preferred solution.

Decision making is independent of data gathering. The data does not make decisions, people do, sometimes with ease and sometimes with difficulty. As we have seen in Part II of this book, individuals and teams apply their own particular viewpoint (their own unique interpretation, prediction and demonstrated preference), often leading to decisions that are severely biased and ultimately flawed. Unless of course they show greater awareness of bias, and apply more careful observation and practice, acted on by informed choice. In other words thinking about our thinking more deeply.

First versus Second Order Thinking

On the basis of our work with leaders, we have observed that good decision makers appear to invest significantly more time engaging in habitual building pattern around their thinking prior to arriving at a decision. They invest more time in second order thinking (see Figure 11.1).

First order thinking relies heavily on what is presented to us (to make a decision), not on how we choose to interpret what is presented to us. In the case of data that is presented to us, we interrogate the data, rarely interrogating how and why we have chosen to see and interpret that data in the way we have. That is to say we rely heavily on data to decide on what we 'see' in a given scenario. However we never question why we see it in that way in the first place. First order thinking more often than not delivers flawed decisions. First order thinking may in fact explain the US-based Center for Creative Leadership's research showing that on average only six out of ten decisions managers make turn out to be the right decision.

Thinking about your thinking

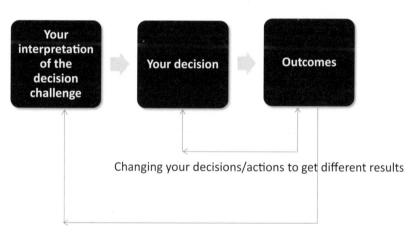

Questioning your own interpretation of the challenge and reframing the challenge

Figure 11.1   First order versus second order decision making

Second order thinking (prior to making a decision) is essentially 'thinking about your thinking'. It recognises that decision making is imprecise and assumes that the examination of your own thinking and the interpretations that thinking is based on is an important and necessary step. Decision making in this case is more deliberate, more mindful.

When we apply this kind of second order thinking habit we are in fact making a conscious choice to interrogate our thinking more deeply. It is this consciousness that improves the quality of decision making. While many of the decisions we make day to day may not require as much deliberate and mindful consideration, there are decisions that have high stakes and are critical to whether we achieve our mission and objectives or not. These will require best practice decision behaviours. We summarise these decision-making behaviours below. While there is often no right answer, adopting and applying these habits more systematically will lead us to the best decision (to be made) for a given set of the circumstances.

Cultural and Contextual Impediments

There are a number of 'cultural' impediments that make a decision process less than ideal. Time-poor managers and leaders torn by the many pressures they experience in a given day may see the need to truncate the time invested to really debate the issues. This inadvertently results in a cursory or superficial discussion. This is especially tough in a singularly task-driven or outcome-driven culture.

Vested interests in an organisation and political play may also often cause people to avoid having the difficult or complex debates that have to be had in order to arrive at a sensible decision. It may even cause a particular framing of the decision that intentionally submerges the real issues that ought to be debated.

Additionally the risk-reward systems in an organisation may not be aligned to collective purpose and this can cause decisions to be taken that are not in the best interests of the broader organisation. These are some, if not all, of the 'cultural' traps that can degrade the quality of the eventual decision.

Furthermore the very structure of organisations can contribute towards the degradation of the quality of decisions. This is because organisations are mostly designed and structured in order to reinforce optimism and remove uncertainty. Smart and knowledgeable people get promoted in organisations and we assume they have all the answers. However when managers are confident about getting the task done without being certain about exactly how – signalling that certainty is foolhardy – then the team is more willing to ask questions. This unleashes a culture where team members are more likely to take the time to be creative, experimental, alert and self-starting. This is in sharp contrast to a culture where mistakes are covered up, and where individuals pretend to be knowledgeable when they are not.

In summary, the culture of the organisation can profoundly contribute to the quality of decision making. Recognising these 'cultural traps' is a good starting point for any decision-making process.

Best Practice Decision Behaviour

Allowing for the cultural impediments described above, a best practice process that leaders can adopt has the following attributes. Obviously it would be quite impractical to apply best practice for every decision you make; instead applying it conscientiously to major high stakes decisions where there is much riding on that decision:

- allocate time:
    - allocate time wisely to the events and issues that are more complex and need greater mindful thinking, that is the higher stakes decisions;
    - take time to separate the facts that have been carefully tested and those that have been assumed – isolate the unchallenged assumptions and scrutinise them more closely;
    - once a decision has been made, postpone further discussion on the decision until a further date to give the group (making the decision) time to develop disagreement and attain a deeper understanding of what the decision is all about, before returning to agree the decision.

- appreciate uncertainty:
    - develop tolerance for uncertainty, variants, deviations, glitches and so on and engage with these in a systematic way;
    - ask all the reasons why this plan of action or decision might be wrong;
    - routinely encourage 'helpful cassandras' who raise difficult questions;
    - pose hypothetical 'what if' questions in order to open up the debate or discussion;
    - as a leader, adopt a style of being 'confidently uncertain'.

- break routines:
    - watch for unthinking routine (heuristics, rules of thumb) and call them out;

- break up natural coalitions – assigning people to tasks on some other basis than traditional loyalties;
- assign a lower-level employee to assume a CEO's or business owner's perspective;
- assign the role of devil's advocate formally so that thinking is disrupted in a legitimate way;
- as a leader absent yourself from early discussions so that you are not swaying perspectives too early in the decision-making process;
- reframe every task in order to 'disrupt' routinised thinking (get a second wind).

- expand your box:
  - seek out and use outsiders, known contrarians or disruptive thinkers imaginatively;
  - foster minority views in order to broaden and deepen debate;
  - switch responsibilities, for example, role reversal, to open up to new/fresh perspective;
  - adopt a mindfully curious approach, staying open and willing to play with ideas you may not be sure will work;
  - catch yourself thinking in binary ways – right or wrong, win or lose, black or white – become comfortable with the grey.

- understand agendas:
  - become alert to personal interest;
  - allow silent beliefs to surface – beliefs that will prevent or frustrate collaboration;
  - watch for win–lose beliefs or zero sum game thinking in the room and challenge respectfully;
  - avoid seeing dissent as disloyalty.

- exercise choice:
  - as a meeting chair, mindfully exercise choice, encouraging a 'greater good' enterprise perspective;
  - ask for alternative solutions, don't stop at the first good solution.

- take distance:
  - take time out to retreat and reassess;
  - debate with yourself;

- be your own devil's advocate;
- find a 'sparring partner' for your ideas/plans.

In addition to this best practice decision-making behaviour there are some blind spots leaders should watch for and these are described below.

Watch for the Blind Spots

Even when armed with best practice decision behaviour, there are blind spots that can derail even the most competent of decision makers amongst us. There are five common blind spots described below.

COMBATING YOUR OVERCONFIDENCE

While recognising that many entrepreneurs are successful because they are overconfident and prepared to take big risks, overconfidence about our own decision-making abilities (explored more fully in Chapter 5) is a major development need that should capture the attention of seasoned and emerging leaders alike.

Centrally, overconfidence can be reduced by considering all the reasons why this answer may be wrong. For example, flag the complex high-stakes decisions where your confidence levels are extreme for extra scrutiny; recalibrate your judgements with those of others, seeking out known contrarians asking why they may be right; treat something that is registering a 90 per cent confidence as though it were 70–75 per cent.

The confidence we have in an expert's advice can be as much a trap as our own confidence. We can't be expert in everything and therefore we learn to trust experts. But experts can get it very wrong. 'I trusted the M&A advisor because I worked with him before on other deals and so I put less energy into vetting his recommendations' is just one scenario that may ring with familiarity. The layman's 'dumb question' can help challenge the overconfidence of an expert. Doctors can also get it wrong. Research shows that the mean time for doctors interrupting the opening statements of patients was after 16.5 seconds and a correlation was found with quality of data collection and accuracy of diagnosis.[2] Except this time this diagnosis may in fact be wrong because they overlooked an additional and critical symptom the patient was showing. This explains why, when confronting patients with complicated medical histories, doctors are often required to consult each other in case they have missed something.

The seeking of a second opinion can also be a useful strategy in combating overconfidence especially when the challenge is a complex one. The second opinion, however, is best sought from someone who has no vested interest in the decision. The more complex the issue the more iterations you need and the more discussion and the more people you need to involve.

SUSPENDING HASTY JUDGEMENT

Strong idea cultures only develop when judgement is suspended. Hasty judgement can kill ideas. This requires us to step away from snap opinions and views when presented with ideas by others. Watch you don't use these instant 'idea killing' phrases (steeped in prejudgement) and coach others who use them:

- 'Yes, but...'

- 'We've tried it before...'

- 'That won't work because...'

- 'Have you really thought about the implications...'

- 'We don't have time for that right now...'

- 'I want to see a cost benefit analysis first...'

- 'OK I hear you but we just invested millions in doing it this other way...'

- 'Fine in theory but it won't work in practice...'

However, holding our judgements at bay is not sufficient. We need childlike curiosity about other views. We have to walk in the other person's shoes – see the world from where they sit even if we think we sit in a better place. You do this by seeking understanding and then nurturing the idea by building on it. Try these lines of questioning driven by genuine child like curiosity:

- Tell me more...

- Help me understand this better...

- Why are you so excited by this idea?

- How is it different?

- What would success look like?

- What would the customer experience?

- What will we need to stop doing to make that work?

- How can we incorporate it into what we do now?

COMBATING THE FRAMING TRAP

A picture can be transformed by changing the frame around it, causing you to see things in that same picture that you had previously not noticed – the intensity of colour, the textures or some other detail. Similarly how a problem or challenge is framed is critical in generating the best decisions. Many decisions turn out to be wrong because of the effects of framing.

Frames can become blinkers. Strategic frames are the mental models that shape how people interpret, for example, their competitive landscape. These models answer questions like 'What business are we in?' or 'Who is the competitor we should fear most.?' In Chapter 2 we discussed the frame that Microsoft used historically to view Apple which led it to underestimating the threat. While frames provide focus they can also blind us. As our success grows, the strategic frames we use grow more rigid and often managers force-fit information into their mental model in order to rationalise why that frame is the right one. They may never actually recognise that the frame is no longer strategically relevant and could even spell disaster for the company. The decline of Firestone and the continued success of Goodyear, both of whom at one point in their history (and before the radial tire technology took off) were in identical positions demonstrates this, Firestone allowed its frame to blindside it, causing it to not abandon the old tyre technology as quickly as Goodyear did. Goodyear benefited from being open and travelling to Europe to learn from the emerging technology being adopted by Michelin. Despite internal resistance it persevered with this new strategic frame. We can all recall framing issues that trapped us into a thinking that later was shown to be flawed.

In order to avoid becoming trapped by routine ways of thinking, hold your own thoughts and judgements lightly, introduce curiosity in your strategic conversations by asking:

- What do we really mean?

- What are we seeing? What are we not seeing?

- What are we assuming?

- What else might we learn?

- Where else could this lead?

Reframing an issue may also be achieved by reversing roles. Role reversal is a commonly used strategy by companies that wish to 'unfreeze' routinised patterns of thinking. It can very effectively bridge the gap between what senior executives think is going on and what line managers know is really going on.

COMBATING GROUP THINK IN YOUR TEAM

It is especially difficult for teams who have worked together for some time to recognise the group think trap. Research undertaken by Irvine Janis[1] summarised the symptoms of group think as follows:

1.   Illusion of Invulnerability: Members ignore obvious danger, take extreme risk, and are overly optimistic.

2.   Collective Rationalisation: Members discredit and explain away warnings contrary to group thinking.

3.   Illusion of Morality: Members believe their decisions are morally correct, ignoring the ethical consequences of their decisions.

4.   Excessive Stereotyping: The group constructs negative stereotypes of rivals outside the group.

5.   Pressure for Conformity: Members pressure others in the group who express arguments against the group's views, viewing such opposition as disloyalty.

6. Self-Censorship: Members withhold their dissenting views and counter-arguments.

7. Illusion of Unanimity: Members perceive falsely that everyone agrees with the group's decision; silence is seen as consent.

8. Mindguards: Some members appoint themselves to the role of protecting the group from adverse information that might threaten group complacency/unity.

There are several tried and tested strategies for combating group think, underscoring the critical role the leader of that group plays, and these include:

- leader adopting a neutral stance when assigning a decision-making task to a group, withholding all preferences and expectations, encourages an atmosphere of open enquiry;

- leader giving priority to airing objections and doubts – more accepting of criticism;

- assigning role of devil's advocate to several strong members of the group;

- dividing the group into two separate deliberative bodies as feasibilities are evaluated;

- inviting outside experts (who have no direct or indirect gain from the decision going either way) and including them in providing decision-making input;

- exploring tentative decisions with trusted others not part of the decision-making group.

COMBATING THE USE OF EXCESSIVE EMOTION

The role of emotion, mood, feeling and so on in decision making is important. When emotions like anger, love, fear or greed are intense they can override our normal cognitive processing causing us to choose poorly or get lost in a dysfunctional loop of indecision. We would point to someone in such a state by saying that they are not in control or just could not help themselves. Apart from 'walking around the block' there are some reflective techniques that can be effective in taking the emotion out of an issue.

For example, when you recognise that your emotions are running high, restore emotional control by asking:

- Am I motivated to see things a certain way?

- What expectation did I bring into the situation?

- Would I see things differently without those expectations and motives?

- Have I consulted with others who don't share my expectation and motives?

In summary, for all of these potential blind spots – whether overconfident or engaged in hasty prejudgement, over-reliance on a particular framing of the issue, swayed by group think or experiencing strong emotion, – 'considering the opposite' can lead to greater accuracy in judgement.

Diagnosing Your Decision-making Style

Over time we all develop a decision-making style – a set of habits that govern how we make decisions. We rarely stand back and reflect on this style. The best way to do this is to periodically review your performance on decisions you have been called upon to make. Look for patterns in the way you make decisions, the logic you use, the experience you rely on, the consultation you engage in, the scrutiny from others you encourage and so on. What does your behaviour tell you about your style? Use the following as a checklist:

- How often do you engage in second order thinking?

- Are your solutions imaginative enough?

- Do you spend too much time on the less important issues?

- Do you tend to gravitate towards choices that, after the fact, seem too conservative?

- Do you tend to miscalculate risk?

- Do you tend to sacrifice thoroughness for speed?

- Do you feel in control of your decision making?

- Are there certain types of people that I engage with or whose opinion I rely on?

To assist you with reviewing, evaluating and modifying your style, and develop best practice decision behaviour, the team at TalentInvest have developed The Decision Maker©, a Decision Styles & Behaviour Diagnostic tool, which you can take by visiting http://www.talentinvest.com.au and following the prompts. This diagnostic tool allows you to self-rate your decision-making style and behaviour along three lines:

- your predispositions in dealing with complexity;

- your predispositions in the decision-making process;

- your actual decision behaviour in the last 12 months.

The diagnostic will help you choose what you wish to change in your decision-making behaviour and in particular how you might refine your technique and style when faced with high-stakes decisions.

Practice makes perfect and all skills can be improved with practice provided it starts with awareness. This diagnostic will give you the awareness you need and will be especially critical when you are faced with significant levels of complexity and anticipate some tough decisions ahead.

Most tough decisions are not as hard as they look. By being systematic you can develop best practice habits and skills which will help you make sounder judgements and better decisions.

Note

1 The Partial Test of Janis's Groupthink Model, C. R. Leana, *Journal of Management*, Spring 1985.

2 The Effect of Physician Solicitation Approaches on Ability to Identify Patient Concerns, L. Dyche MSW and D. Swiderski MD, *Journal of General Internal Medicine*, March 2005.

12

The Future of Decision Making

Faced with profound macro-level changes in the business and societal context, decision making will inevitably evolve in the coming years and our decision behaviour and style will have to adapt with it.

Discontinuous change, new technologies, generational differences in decision behaviour, the post Global Financial Crisis (GFC) business dynamic and with it the centrality of the stakeholder (in contrast to decades of shareholder primacy), and of course globalisation will impact the way the decision-making process is perceived and is experienced. Although we take these forces of change individually, their complex interplay creates a truly challenging backdrop for decision making in the future. The changes we describe below will profoundly influence the way we compensate for all or some of the influences of the eight biases explored in Part II.

Discontinuous Change and Reduced Visibility

Our visibility of the future is declining while the pace of change in our economies and cultures is accelerating, fuelled, but not exclusively, by new technologies. Predicting what will happen next is now much harder. Uncertainty has taken hold not only in boardrooms but in offices, cubicles, meeting hubs and coffee shops everywhere, as executives and employees struggle with core questions: How sustainable is our business model? Which competitive advantages have staying power? What skills matter most? How to weigh the opportunities and threats when the fundamentals of your business may change overnight?

Just five years ago, three companies controlled 64 per cent of the Smartphone market: Nokia, Research in Motion and Motorola. Today, two different companies are at the top of the industry: Samsung and Apple. This sudden complete swap in the pecking order of a global multibillion-dollar industry is not unique. Chaos is here to stay and not simply from the disruption created by the often-quoted technology-related companies like Apple, Facebook and Google. No one predicted that massive book chains like Borders or Waterstones would fall like bowling pins. No one predicted that General Motors would become bankrupt and then come back from the abyss with greater momentum than Toyota.

However, for those of us in search of a road map or model that will define the next era, there is no credible long-term picture of the future. There is one certainty only. The next decade or two will be defined not by any new business model but by more fluidity and more ambiguity, making sound decision must more challenging to achieve. If there is a pattern to all this, it is that there is no pattern at all and organisations need to develop a special resilience in order to thrive in this new world. Most large organisations are good at solving clear but complicated problems. They are not great at solving ambiguous problems – when you don't know what you don't know. Faced with ambiguity, many organisational systems will struggle with the decisions they are called on to make.

The impact this has on decision making is that information may have less relevance and decision makers will have to learn to cope with greater levels of ambiguity, which may be uncomfortable for some. Learning the skills to be comfortable with and working with unprecedented levels of ambiguity will be increasingly critical for leaders everywhere. Learning agility in other words will become a distinguishing attribute of outstanding decision makers.

Decision Making in a Globalised World

Today, there are few large businesses that don't aspire to play globally, accessing the global market as a source for procurement, a basis for manufacturing and to market their products, even if not intending to set up operations globally. Even small businesses are feeling the impact of globalisation of markets and customers. Globalisation will bring on the need for decision makers everywhere to have some level of cross-cultural intelligence and comfort with diversity. On the other hand it will homogenise/converge information, knowledge, skills and methodologies. For example, increasingly teams comprise decision makers with decision behaviour and styles that are drawn from different cultural backgrounds, each with a different attitude to power distance, a different risk appetite, a different relational attitude and so on. This would add complexity to the decision-making process.

This complexity will not only show itself in the speed in which decisions are made, but also in the underpinning values, the extent to which stakeholders are engaged in the process of making the decision and the way in which decisions once made are communicated. Nowhere is this more stark than in a multinational company that has to roll out a programme of change across the multiple countries it operates in, which will call for transcultural sensitivity, fluency and agility.

In making decisions, the relevance of experience and expertise honed in home markets will need to be examined more closely and so will our attachment to policies and practices that we have come to rely on. Local markets require local expertise. The well-worn *Think Global Act Local* slogan has been a challenge for many global companies who, despite the intent, default to their attachment to a singular global approach argued on the basis of efficiency but more often also driven by fear of an unknown world 'out there'. In particular, globalisation requires a resetting of core values and beliefs as well as an unlearning and relearning of new skills, acquiring new knowledge about markets, cultural nuances and business practices. The impact on the decision-making process of these changes will be profound.

Furthermore, the opening up of the markets and the interconnectedness of the markets has meant that decisions made in one part of the globe will now have a sometimes immediate impact on another. This connectivity has significant implications for the range of thinking skills and styles that decision makers increasingly need to apply. Systemic thinking is essential, only the system is bigger and more global.

A New Generation of Decision Makers

In 2025, the current Gen Y will be the leaders in our organisations. This is an uber-confident generation big on immediate gratification, high on mobility and who operate with less clear work–play boundaries. This will surely herald a different set of work values which will drive how institutions and businesses are run and in turn how decisions are made.

Additionally the dimming lure of the large company and the attraction of a freer, more open entrepreneurial environment will have greater appeal and with it less systematised thinking. While baby boomers (BB) may complain about the short attention spans of Gen Y, this multitasking ease may in fact create more nimble and agile decision makers.

The tendency to experiment with careers rather than stick with a single path and accumulate deep expertise in a single 30–40-year career is a well-documented characteristic of Gen Y. This type of career, while delivering less depth, will deliver greater breadth of experience. Gen Y is more likely to hop in and out of multiple careers paths, trying their hand at being employed as well as self-employed. This has an implication on how they will make decisions and choices. Their level of attachment to ideas or paradigms or models will be weaker than the current BB generation. Their ability to challenge what the BB generation has taken for granted or been trapped by is likely to result in a greater level of creativity and innovation in solutions they come up with.

The fact that Gen Y are on average better travelled than their parents and nearly a third of under 30s are working in a country they did not get their degree in means this generation will be more exposed to cross-cultural perspectives and will be more likely to embrace diversity more readily.

Gen Y's reported deeper preoccupation with the search for meaning and purpose may also result in a new generation of decision makers who are less preoccupied with making wealth than sharing it. It will also result in decisions being tested for their relevance to broader societal purpose rather than just the profit purpose.

The Post Global Finanical Crisis Business Dynamic and Primacy of Stakeholder

Hindsight is a wonderful thing and we can all now see how decision makers intoxicated with optimism contributed to the collapse of major parts of the banking and financial system, now often referred to as the GFC.

The term 'the new normal' has been used to describe the era of no or low growth that many countries and companies, saddled with debt and declining revenues, now experience. The questioning of capitalism in its current form, recognition of the limitations of shareholder primacy and short-term profiteering has also been accompanied by anger and rage on the streets about the excesses of businesses. The bonus culture is also perceived as being one of the major causes of the crash. Today companies need to apply a wider lens to the very definition of corporate success and examine the issue of profit versus profiteering. What is certain is that the time when the shareholder was all powerful is long gone and the need for decision makers to think about and factor in the needs of all of its stakeholders is here.

We are beginning to experience a period not dissimilar to that following the Great Depression in the 1930s where businesses were actively de-risked and companies and individuals lived frugally. This lower risk appetite is evidenced in the large amounts of cash that companies are now currently sitting on. It is also evidenced by the reluctance of banks to loan even to the safest of businesses, reluctance of companies to invest in retraining and re-skilling for longer-term competitiveness even in booming and continuously growing markets such as China. Cost containment and a more insular home turf protection appears to be the name of the post GFC game.

It will be many years, even decades, before the long dark shadow of the GFC is erased from the decision maker's mind and management teams will return to the decision-making confidence, optimism and hope shown before the GFC, minus of course the hubris, complacency and the overconfidence that marked the period that went before.

The Impact of New Technologies

Technology has brought, and will continue to bring change, to the way we live and work, behave and even think. Technology has been a key driver of innovation and hence growth. In light of fast technological innovation, our personal and professional lives have never been as much influenced and determined as it is today by technology.

Technology is continually challenging our core beliefs, for example of how markets operate or how the consumer decides. It has given reason for increased optimism as well as increased apprehension in decision makers. New technologies are redrawing the map of the competitive landscape and consequently can profoundly change a company's capacity to grow and the decision maker's ability to predict.

In anticipation of the benefits of technology, as decision makers we can sometimes optimistically overestimate what technology can do for our businesses. On the other hand we can also underestimate the power of technology and the way it can transform our markets and threaten our traditional businesses. Business literature is littered with examples, for example in the retail sector of companies that underestimated the power of online shopping. Retail traders in the high street wait optimistically for the recession to lift and for shoppers to return to the high street but they won't – many have left for the online highway with no intention to return soon.

However, it would be a gross omission in this section to not raise the impact of new developments in Artificial Intelligence (AI) and speculate on its impact on the future of decision making. Speculation is all it will be because the science is continuing to evolve. The AI field was founded on the claim that a central property of humans, intelligence, can be precisely simulated by a machine. AI appears to have successfully simulated human intelligence in simple problems requiring logical deductions. However more complex challenges has eluded AI advances to date.

Most of the AI algorithms in use today to solve complex problems will require an amount of memory and computer time that makes it unfeasible to try and model. Much of what people know is not represented as 'facts' or 'statements' that they could express verbally, but instead they are complex intuitions. For example, a chess master will avoid a particular chess position because it 'feels too exposed' or an art critic can take one look at a sculpture or painting and instantly realise that it is a fake. These are complex intuitions or tendencies that are represented in the brain unconsciously but represent knowledge that informs, supports and provides a context for symbolic, conscious knowledge. Almost nothing in complex decision making today is simply true or false in the way that abstract logic requires. AI research continues to explore a number of solutions to this problem of simulating the more intuitive 'secret life' of human decision making with the hope that complex decision making can one day be simulated by computers, inserting more objectivity into decision making. AI, now very much part of the field of technology, will continue in its relentless march to simulate decision scenarios that will assist the decision maker in the future.

Implications for Leaders Everywhere

Faced with many unknowables and our somewhat brief and speculative journey in this chapter about the 'future state', the one thing we can conclude is that as leaders we need to get better at decisions. This means urgently investing in our decision-making behaviour and decision competence. We need to become more sophisticated decision makers and acquire the skills required in an increasingly uncertain, volatile and ambiguous world.

And finally, whatever the 'future state', decision makers cannot rely on what made them successful in the past. They will need to learn to exercise choices wisely by becoming more thoughtful and more agile simultaneously.

Index

Other titles you might be interested in from Gower

Business Wargaming
Daniel F. Oriesek and Jan Oliver Schwarz
ISBN: 978-0-566-08837-7

Choosing Leaders and Choosing to Lead
Douglas Board, Cass Business School, City University, London
ISBN: 978-1-4094-3648-5

Decision Sourcing
Dale Roberts and Rooven Pakkiri
ISBN: 978-1-4094-4247-9

Escalation in Decision-Makingy
Helga Drummond and Julia Hodgson
ISBN: 978-1-4094-0236-7

Exploiting Future Uncertainty
David Hillson
ISBN: 978-1-4094-2341-6

Game Theory in Management
Michael Hatfield
ISBN: 978-1-4094-4241-7

HyperThinking
Philip Weiss
ISBN: 978-1-4094-2845-9

MisLeadership
John Rayment, Anglia Ruskin and Jonathan Smith
ISBN: 978-0-566-09226-8

Rethinking Management
Chris Mowles
ISBN: 978-1-4094-2933-3

GOWER